Prayer, Power & Petticoats

D1016661

Sue Tennant
2005

9.24.16.28.20

Phyllis Lundvall
Bonnie Earhart

Prayer, Power & Petticoats

Lessons in Faith from the First Ladies

From Martha Washington to Laura Bush

by Sue E. Tennant

Bridge-Logos

Gainesville, FL 32614 USA

Prayer, Power & Petticoats
Lessons in Faith From the First Ladies
by Sue E. Tennant

Copyright ©2004 by Bridge-Logos
Library of Congress Catalog Card Number pending
International Standard Book Number 0-88270-800-7

Published by:

Bridge-Logos

P.O. Box 141630
Gainesville, FL 32614 USA
bridgelogos.com

Printed in the United States of America. All rights reserved. Under International Copyright Law, no part of this publicaiton may be reproduced, stored, or transmitted by any means—elecronic, mechanical, photographic (photocopy), recording, or otherwise—without written permission from the Publisher.

Dedication

For my mother
Sarah Hill Leslie
in her 100th year of being the
First Lady in our family.

Acknowledgments

I owe it all to a wild and wonderful lady I met one evening in a church meeting and felt after one hour that I had known her all of my life. Her dedication to her art, her compassion and her drive are unmatched in the literary field. Without Bev Browning, there would be no lessons from the First Ladies. The staff of the National First Ladies' Education and Research Center were also invaluable in their assistance and support for the research in this book: Mary Regula, President and Founding Chair; Dr. Sheila Fisher, Vice President and interior designer ("Pink is our beige."); Pat Krider, Executive Director; Lucinda Frailly, Educational Director ("Cindy"); Barbara Hickman, Building Facilities Manager (US Army, Retired); Sheila Lolli, Operations Coordinator for Tours. I would also like to thank Sally Buck and Dianne Walsh for research assistance and encouragement; Melisa Durden, Scriptural Editor; and designer Elizabeth Nason who turned a pile of typing paper into tender portraits of the First Ladies as she built this book.

Special thanks to Dr. Craig Schermer, Archivist, Historian, and Librarian at the National First Ladies' Education and Research Center, for his generosity, passion, talent, and knowledge so deep and wide that it redefines human capacity.

And finally a big thank you to my husband, Jeff, children Matt and Bethany, and my family and friends for putting up with months of First Lady trivia and tales.

Contents

Introduction

Relax. The country is in good hands. There's a woman in the White House. The First Ladies of the United States are an exclusive sorority of great women who contribute significantly to the success of their husbands' administrations. But they do it without getting paid, without being trained, sometimes without agreeing to this career move, and without acknowledgement. Most of their work with the presidents is private, but every flub is public. Once a First Lady crossed the threshold of the White House, she belongs to a nation.

When I began this book I wondered what we, 21st century women, could learn from a succession of women who lived ... and live ... in a mansion with servants on duty twenty-four hours a day. As it turned out, quite a lot.

Allow me to introduce you to a surprising source of heritage and tradition for wives and mothers. I want you to meet the First Ladies. We are all familiar with our forefathers. Now it's time to get to know the women who stood behind and beside the most powerful men in our country, bore their children, managed their homes, hosted their parties, entertained their dignitaries, handled their press and public relations, did their laundry, straightened their ties, and partnered with them to build the United States of America.

Just in case you were thinking that First Ladies are gracious hostesses, and that the presidents are fully capable of running the country and the White House independently, remember that no president has ever been able to function without a First Lady. In every case where the president has been a bachelor or a widower, he has found it necessary to recruit the assistance of a generous woman. No man is president alone. He HAS to have a helpmate. It is no accident that the president's family lives in the same building from which he runs the country. As one First Lady so aptly put it, "It's a little like living above the family store." Another First Lady remarked how it was hard not to get involved in politics because "my husband works at home." It's critical for a president to have his helpmate close at hand at all times. The vice president might be just a heartbeat away from the presidency, but the First Lady is a heartbeat away from the president.

So what do we women who are married to non-presidents have to learn from First Ladies? Lots. You would be surprised at how much we have in common with them, and how much they have to teach us. The First Ladies of the United States are extraordinary in their ordinariness, so if you are looking for a mentoring woman who is like you, and has mastered the art and science of being an ultimate helpmate, there is no better place to look than the White House. In fact, First Ladies of long ago, perceived as quietly powerful and secretly a lot more politically astute than demure, were called "Petticoat Presidents."

If the First Lady is the power behind the president, who is the power behind the First Lady? God. The United States is "One Nation Under God," and that trust in God begins in the White House. From the first day of the new republic to this very morning, there has been prayer in the White House. Some days "God help us" may be the most common phrase heard in the building! From Martha to Laura, prayer has played a dominant and consistent role in daily White House routine run by Prayer, Power, and Petticoats.

Although coming from diverse backgrounds upon entering the White House, First Ladies experience the same trials and triumphs that you and I do. We see their triumphs. They are many. But the White House does not provide immunity from scandal, drugs, infidelity, disease, sorrow, or death. First Ladies, uniquely human, have dealt with life in a wide range of ways. Some accepted things; some struggled. Some enjoyed the challenge; some retreated to bed for a while. But the one thing that sustained them was faith. Their strength helped hold families together in spite of incredible pressures. To date no White House couple has divorced after their term of office. Perhaps if a couple can survive the White House, they can survive anything. There are valuable lessons in getting to know the First Ladies and how they supported their husbands and maintained strong marriages throughout all that life could throw at them.

In each section of this book, you'll find a short biography of each of these ordinary, extraordinary First Ladies. You'll get to know her a little and see how she affected and influenced her husband's career. At the end of each section, I've provided Scripture that suits her. I've added a short commentary on the lessons in faith that we can learn from her. Where possible, I've used her own words. But many of the First Ladies, particularly the early ones who lived in a time when women were seen and not heard, left no papers or letters, so it's impossible to know exactly where they stood on specific matters of faith. When there are no surviving documents, I've merely observed the First Lady's faith in action and pointed out lessons. Each First Lady's section concludes with my short prayer that reflects facets of faith that are her signature.

You are about to meet wonderful wives and mothers who have much to teach us about family and faith. Allow me to introduce you to the First Ladies of the United States of America.

I hope you enjoy the experience.
Sue Tennant

Proverbs 31

10 Who can find a virtuous woman? For her price is far above rubies.

11 The heart of her husband does safely trust in her, so that he shall have no need or spoil.

12 She will do him good and not evil all the days of her life.

13 She seeks wool, and flax, and works willingly with her hands.

14 She is like the merchants' ships; she brings her food from afar.

15 She rises also while it is yet night, and gives meat to her household, and a portion to her maidens.

16 She considers a field, and buys it: with the fruit of her hands she plants a vineyard.

17 She girds her loins with strength, and strengthens her arms.

18 She perceives that her merchandise is good; her candle goes not out by night.

19 She lays her hand on the spindle, and her hands hold the distaff.

20 She stretches out her hand to the poor; yes, she reaches forth her hands to the needy.

21 She is not afraid of the snow for her household; for all her household are clothed with scarlet.

22 She makes herself coverings of tapestry; her clothing is silk and purple.

23 Her husband is known in the gates, when he sits among the elders of the land.

24 She makes fine linen, and sells it; and delivers girdles unto the merchant.

25 Strength and honor are her clothing; and she shall rejoice in time to come.

26 She opens her mouth with wisdom; and in her tongue is the law of kindness.

27 She looks well to the ways of her household, and eats not the bread of idleness.

28 Her children arise up, and call her blessed; her husband also, and he praises her.

29 Many daughters have done virtuously, but you excel them all.

30 Favor is deceitful, and beauty is van; but a woman that fears the LORD, she shall be praised.

31 Give her of the fruit of her hands; and let her own works praise her in the gates.

1

Martha Dandridge Custis Washington

"I have learned from experience that the greater part of our happiness or misery depends on our dispositions and not on our circumstances." Martha Washington

Meet Martha

Born	Virginia, 1731
Married	Daniel Custis, 1749
	George Washington, 1759
Children	Four (two died in infancy, one at 17 and one at 27)
First Lady	1789-1797
Died	1802 at age 70
Martha's World	First U.S. capital established in New York, first president of the United States, first First Lady, first national bank opened, first mint founded . . . first almost everything.

In 1783, at the age of 51, Martha Washington was overjoyed to return to Mt. Vernon and retire with her husband. It wasn't a real retirement since she still had to raise two grandchildren, manage a large plantation, entertain hundreds of friends and acquaintances, cook, weave, pay the bills, and care for her husband. But it was a vast improvement over living in huts and temporary houses during the Revolutionary War, where she darned socks, made bandages, cared for wounded soldiers and struggled through the mud and ice of Philadelphia and Valley Forge. Mt. Vernon from 1783 to 1789 was a pleasant time, but it was only a short lull in a hard and oftentimes sorrowful life for Martha.

In 1789, at the age of 57, Martha Washington had to begin a new career as our first "First Lady." She didn't want to leave Mt. Vernon, but the young country desperately needed George Washington as its first President, so she bundled up some belongings, her two grandchildren, and a few servants, and moved to New York. The trip was long and the weather did not cooperate. She actually missed the first inauguration and inaugural ball. Upon her arrival, she would have no rest, since her husband had already scheduled a large dinner for the next afternoon. Thus started eight years of receptions, dinners, callings, and entertainment that drained the energy and the resources of our first presidential

While in New York, the Washingtons lived for some time in this house on Cherry Street.

couple. They lived in small houses in New York and Philadelphia, our first two capitol cities, during Washington's two terms in office. Washington declined to run a third term, setting a precedent that lasted for 144 years. They never lived in Washington or the White House.

Born in Virginia, Martha received little education beyond the domestic skills expected of a good and dutiful wife-to-be. And following the established protocol of colonial Virginia, she married at age 18 to a wealthy planter almost twenty years her senior. She had four children; two who died in infancy. Her husband died in 1757, leaving her a widow at age 26 with two young children. She met and married George Washington in 1759. The few letters that remain show a very considerate and smitten young George; and the fact that Martha was a very wealthy young widow with 17,000 acres of land probably didn't hurt her potential as a good candidate for life partner. Her mild and gentle nature aside, Martha followed husband General George into service to their country: onto the battlegrounds of the Revolutionary War... all the way to the White House. Her two children lived with them, but her daughter died of epilepsy in 1773, and her son died of fever in 1781. Her son left a wife and four children, and George and Martha adopted the two youngest and raised them as their own.

Martha entered the "President's House" not knowing what to do, what to wear, what to serve, when to appear in public, or when to disappear. She had no role model and no instructions. But Martha had successfully managed a large plantation for years and quickly assumed the role of our nation's first hostess with charm and dignity. She took no personal interest in politics, but devoted her life to her husband and family. She wrote of that time, "I think I am more like a state prisoner than anything else, there is certain bounds set for me which I must not depart from." Although criticized by some for being too regal and by others for being too common, Lady Washington was loved and admired by most for being a gentle, kind spirit, and always gracious and courteous.

After the presidency, the Washingtons returned to Mt. Vernon for two peaceful years before George, her dear friend and companion of 40 years, passed away. Martha lived another two and a half years before dying in 1802 of fever at the age of 70.

Martha was raised in the Church of England and attended St. Peter's Church as a child. She also brought up her children and grandchildren in the church and regularly read her Bible. One reference indicates that her daughter-in-law, Nellie, used to read the Psalms to her or sing her favorite hymns when Martha retired each evening at 9:00 o'clock.

During the Revolutionary War, Martha traveled north each winter to be with her husband wherever his troops were barracked for the season. One winter they were in Cambridge and she was dismayed to discover that the old Christ Church had been boarded up and abandoned. At Martha's request, the church was reopened and restored in time for a New Year's Day church service.

A participant wrote that it was a moving service with the soldiers escorting General Washington into the church with fife and drum and the little church resonating with the strong voices of the men singing hymns. When the chaplain read from Psalms 118 and 119, it brought tears to many eyes. A viola and clarinet provided music, because they could not use the organ. The pipes had long been pulled out and turned into ammunition.

When she was dying with the fever, Martha sent for her clergyman and received last communion. Although we know little of her formal religion, we know her faith from her actions. Despite the loss of a husband and four children, she never gave up hope. Although it would have been easy for her to assume the role of a cultured lady, sipping tea and giving parties, she went to Valley Forge to support her husband, her soldiers, and her new country. She was our first First Lady, and set an example of compassion and caring for all the First Ladies who followed.

Lessons from Martha

I called upon the Lord in distress: the Lord answered me and set me in a large place. The Lord is on my side: I will not fear: what can man do unto me? The Lord taketh my part with them that help me: therefore shall I see my desire upon them that hate me. It is better to trust in the Lord than to put confidence in man. It is better to trust in the Lord than to put confidences in princes (Psalm 118:5-9).

And I will walk at liberty: for I seek thy precepts. I will speak of thy testimonies also before kings, and will not be ashamed (Psalm 119: 45-46).

Of the hundreds of lessons we might learn from Martha, perhaps the most important is the consistency of the Word of God. We read Psalms 118 and 119, and ponder the words just as Martha and George and that small band of revolutionary soldiers did more than 220 years ago. The same words, the same prayers, the same hymns are still being sung today in chapels, and barracks, in churches, and cathedrals the world over.

The choice of Scripture for that cold New Year's Day in 1776 is certainly prophetic. The new republic needed God's help. They needed reassurance that the Lord was on their side. They needed to "seek liberty" from kings and princes. The war was not going well; losses were high, and supplies and new recruits were low. Washington lamented that they were in a dire predicament. He thought that if they were somehow to rise above, it would have to be with the help of the "finger of Providence" blinding the eyes of the enemy to the disadvantages of the Revolutionary Army. Perhaps that one New Year's Day church service, spearheaded by Martha, provided the small spark needed to recharge the army and eventually save the republic. The whole "Hand of Providence" was guiding the republic, as it does today. For each time we open our Bibles, we are being recharged and raised up to "walk in liberty" along God's path.

Dear God, thank you for being the same today as yesterday, as last year, as 200 and 2000 years ago. May we always find the same comfort and guidance in your Scriptures as our fathers and forefathers before us. Amen.

2

Abigail Smith Adams

"I really believe they (the British) are more afraid of the Americans' prayers than their swords." Abigail Adams

Meet Abigail

Born	Massachusetts, 1744
Married	John Adams, 1764
Children	Five (one died in infancy)
First Lady	1797–1801
Died	1818 at age 73
Abigail's World	The Capitol moves to Washington from Philadelphia; smallpox vaccinations are offered for the first time; the second US census shows a population of 5.3 million; 4-tined forks replace the old 2 and 3-tined forks for dining.

Abigail Adams wrote letters virtually every day of her life, and more than 2,000 of them remain in historical archives for us to read. It's important to remember that the early First Ladies had little sense of their place and importance in history, so their personal papers and correspondence, if there were any at all, were not carefully retained. Abigail Adams was the exception. Her letters remain not only to give us a fascinating chronicle of daily life as a president's wife, but, more important, to allow us a glimpse into her personal, inner life of faith and intellect.

That she left letters at all is remarkable. Born in an age when society didn't believe that women needed formal education, Abigail taught herself to read and write from her father's and grandfather's libraries. She wasn't a generation ahead of her time ... she was two centuries ahead of her time. Not only did she teach herself, but she taught her children, and later even studied French and Latin so she could instruct them.

Abigail Adams is welcomed by her husband John as she arrives at the still-unfinished White House. The couple lived there for the last four months of his term.

Her relationship with God and her education as a Christian began at birth. Born in Massachusetts in 1744, she was the daughter of Reverend William Smith, the pastor of the Congregational Church in Weymouth.

In 1764 at the old age of almost 20, she married John Adams, then 29. Their letters to each other and historical accounts from outside sources reveal a devoted marriage of 54 years. They had five children, four of whom lived to adulthood. Just as in some families today, Abigail and John's parenting skills yielded a wide range in results— from black sheep to shining star and everything in between. One son died an alcoholic, and one became the sixth President of the United States.

A young Abigail Adams is shown here on a Revolutionary War era collectible plate.

John and Abigail's married life was entwined with war: first the French and Indian War, then the Revolutionary War, and then the British and French War. In 1778, John Adams was assigned to Paris as commissioner. John and Abigail were separated for more than six years. Because transportation between the United States and Europe was by ship — then a slow, treacherous voyage — sometimes there would be no mail or word of any kind for months at a time. John beseeched Abigail for years to join him. Finally in 1784, she relented and made the trip to France. She returned a mere four years later, scandalized and appalled by the French. She was too much a Puritan to accept, much less enjoy, the "immoralities" and "indecencies" of European culture.

Shortly after returning from abroad, Adams was elected the first Vice President of the United States under George Washington and in 1797 was elected our second president. Abigail maintained an active political role with her husband both in Philadelphia, then the capital of the United States, and when they moved into the new White House in the new town of Washington, in 1800.

Abigail was not only the First Lady, with duties to fulfill on her husband's behalf, but she was also a wife and mother with a new home to set up and maintain for her family. One would think that the glamour of a presidential mansion would have been generous compensation for the inconvenience of uprooting and moving her family again, but unfortunately the "President's House" wasn't finished when they moved in. Not one room was plastered, and there were no bells, no plumbing and no stairway to the second floor. The plans (drawn by an architect who obviously wanted to depict a grand governmental building instead of a home) contained no facilities for a laundry. One of the first duties of the White House's first First Lady, Abigail Adams, was to hang wet laundry in the unfinished East Room.

Abigail and grandaughter Suzanna supervise as servant hangs wash in the East Room.

A lesser woman would have despaired of the disorganization and difficulties of the emerging new capital, Washington. But not Abigail. The town itself was "a quagmire after every rain," but she, always trying to find some positive point to report, noted that the President's House had a great view of the Potomac.

"I think we have too many high sounding words and too few actons that correspond with them."
Abigail Adams

Over 200 years later, Abigail is still regarded as one of our finest First Ladies. Although criticized by some as having too much influence over the President, she was indisputably a true partner and trusted advisor to Adams. She was not a feminist in the modern sense of the term, but Abigail believed in the equality of the sexes. She was the one who advised her husband to "remember the ladies" in drafting the new Constitution. She was also very clear about the importance of a wife's role: "No man ever prospered in the world without the consent and cooperation of his wife."

Abigail had an intense faith that guided her in all of her duties. Through their long separations, Abigail recorded that she had little but God to console her. She made her confession of faith in 1759 at the age of 15, and remained a very devoted and pious believer until her death. She participated in days of fasting and prayer during the wars. She put her religion and her position as First Lady into action by advocating quality education for women and blacks.

Certain of what was right, she was never afraid to speak out for her beliefs. Almost 100 years before the Civil War, Abigail enrolled one of her two black servants in a local school. When a townsman objected, Abigail replied, "The boy is a freeman as much as any of the young men, and merely because his face is black, is he to be denied instruction, how is he to be qualified to procure a livelihood? Is this the Christian principle of doing to others as we would have others to do us? ... I have not thought it any disgrace to my self to take him into my parlour and teach him both to read and write... I hope we shall all go to Heaven together."

Lessons from Abigail

Great is my boldness of speech toward you, great is my glorying of you, I am filled with comfort (2 Corinthinans 7:4).

From Abigail we can learn courage and boldness. She never backed down from writing or speaking out for what was right and good. Abigail was a strict mother and a very stern and opinionated mother-in-law, but she had the courage to step out of the traditional wife and mother roles and speak out for what she believed, even when she was definitely in the minority. Who else was championing for racial and gender equality in the 18th century? Women could not even own property and our young nation had 800,000 slaves. She was not a radical, just an educated woman who saw God's spirit in everyone, regardless of their color, age or gender.

Dear God, give us the strength and the courage to stand up and speak out when action is needed. Remind us that silence and inaction are sometimes just as sinful as unjust words or acts. Amen.

3

Martha Wayles Skelton Jefferson

"Time wastes too fast: every letter I trace tells me with what rapidity life follows my pen."
Poem by Laurence Sterne that Martha copied on her deathbed

Jefferson's daughter, Martha ("Patsy") sometimes served as hostess during his adminiatration.

Meet Martha

Born	Virginia, 1748
Married	Bathurst Skelton, 1766
	Thomas Jefferson, 1772
Children	One son by Skelton
	Six by Jefferson (four died in childhood)
First Lady	Died 19 years before Jefferson took office
Died	1782 at the age of 33
Martha's World	Benjamin Franklin invents the lightning rod; the Revolutionary War ends; Harvard Medical School opens.

Thomas Jefferson's wife Martha never had the opportunity to serve as First Lady. By the time President Jefferson entered the White House in 1801, his beloved wife had been deceased almost 20 years. He entered alone with his exotic plants, his violin, and his pet mockingbird. His was a quiet administration, more about getting down to business than about entertaining or being entertained. He declined most social engagements, and when he had guests at the White House, he preferred small, informal dinners. When a hostess was needed, he asked one of his two daughters or Dolley Madison to preside over the festivities. He never remarried.

No picture of Martha Jefferson exists, although she is described as small and beautiful. She was a widow when Jefferson met her; and when her father died a few years later, she became a very wealthy woman. No correspondence exists between Martha and Jefferson, but their daughters' writings describe a loving and happy marriage. Martha played the piano and he the violin, and they spent their evenings playing duets and singing. Unfortunately, Martha had six pregnancies in their ten years of marriage. Only two daughters survived to adulthood. Each pregnancy took a toll on her health. In fact, she died just four months after her last child was born.

During their marriage, Jefferson stayed home as much as possible and declined a governmental appointment in Paris because of his wife's poor health. When she died, he was overcome with grief and did not leave his room for three weeks. His daughter said that he broke his seclusion with long rides on horseback, still wracked by sorrow. He kept a small silhouette of Martha and a lock of her hair, but all other reminders and mementos of his wife were destroyed.

We know nothing of her faith other than to assume that she was of the Anglican Church.

Lessons from Martha

"So teach us to number our days, that we may apply our hearts unto wisdom." Psalm 90:12

She was known by only those who lived during her time and loved her, but we can sense her spirit by her husband's devotion. For such a great and learned man to feel such happiness during their marriage and such despair upon her death suggests that she was a wonderful person. Jefferson would have been a challenging spouse, so it would have taken an unusual woman to hold her own in that relationship.

The first lesson we learn from her is that life is short, so we must live and love fully every day we are here. There are few who can predict the end of their days, so it behooves us all to make the most of the days we are given.

Martha's other lesson is that when a woman surrounds her family in love, rears her children so well that they can step into her shoes, and equips her husband with the confidence and tenderness necessary for greatness, she leaves a heritage: a lasting legacy of accomplishment that can resonate for generations.

Dear God, let this day be Your day. Help us to fill this day with joy and giving, never postponing goodness. Amen.

4
❦

Dorothea (Dolley) Payne Todd Madison

"Nature never intended me for obscurity." Dolley Madison

Meet Dolley

Born	North Carolina, 1768
Married	John Todd, 1790 (died of yellow fever in 1793)
	James Madison, 1794
Children	Two by John Todd (one died in infancy)
First Lady	1809-1817
Died	1849 at the age of 81
Dolley's World	Congress declares war on Britain in the War of 1812; the *Star-Spangled Banner* is written during one of the naval battles; Yale Medical School opens.

Although James Madison served as President of the United States for eight years, Dolley Madison, his wife, served as Washington's most famous hostess for over 30 years. She greeted and feted kings, queens, farmers and friends during the administrations of six presidents.

Dolley Madison was a legend in her own time, and remarkably 200 years later she is still one of the best known and most admired of the First Ladies. She honed her superb hostess skills while her husband, James Madison, served as Secretary of State for eight years. By the time she took over the White House in 1809, she was well equipped to turn a staid and stately house into a colorful and festive place.

Dolley was born into a large Quaker family in North Carolina, and married a young Quaker lawyer when she was 21. They had two sons. Unfortunately, an epidemic of yellow fever claimed her husband and one infant son in 1793.

At age 25, Dolley was a widowed mother, but being on her own wouldn't last. Before long, she had many suitors. She chose and married James Madison in 1794, a man who was willing to be both husband and instant father. One can only surmise that the decision to marry a non-Quaker was a difficult one, because marriage outside of the Quaker faith meant she was exiled. And so it was. The new Mrs. Madison was summarily dismissed from the Society of Friends.

For everything lost, something is gained. For Dolley, giving up membership as a Quaker meant that life blossomed. She went from the gray and brown of the Quakers to flowered gowns, colorful turbans, flamboyant feathers and glittering jewelry. Even before her husband became president, Dolley served as First Lady for Thomas Jefferson, whose own wife died 19 years before he took office. Jefferson needed a hostess, and Dolley never missed an opportunity to entertain.

Near the end of the War of 1812, British troops set fire to the White House. Dolley Madison bravely salvaged what she could, including the famous Gilbert Stuart portrait of George Washington (below), the only object in the President's House since the time of its first occupancy in 1800.

When James Madison became President, Dolley's well practiced grand receptions ("crushes") were the height of the social scene in Washington, D.C. But as much fun as they were, there was profound political purpose to them. Dolley was a true helpmate to James, and did much to compensate for his short stature and retiring nature—qualities that would certainly make it difficult for heads of state and common folk alike to see James Madison as an effective and dynamic leader, even though he was more than capable.

Dolley, glamorous and gregarious, engineered "a presence" for him at these receptions. Since James was only five feet, four inches tall, and weighed barely 100 pounds, the president was easily lost in the crowd. Dolley lovingly called him "The Great Little Madison." She, in her towering turbans (one feathered creation supposedly caught fire in a chandelier), would circulate through the room and maneuver each important guest through the throng to her husband's side, where the two of them could talk. Dolley had an extraordinary ability to remember names and faces, so introductions were never awkward. Once the president and his guest were comfortably chatting, she would leave the two of them and return to the crowd to spot and shepherd her next target. By the end of the evening, James, without having to move and completely invisible over the heads of the guests, would have spoken with everyone in the room.

Unfortunately, it was during Madison's term in office that the War of 1812 broke out, and Dolley had to flee the White House just hours before it was burned by the British. In the now famous story, she waited until she could see the smoke from the British cannons before she grabbed the portrait of George Washington, trunks of historical documents, and her pet macaw and raced out of Washington in a carriage. The White House was burned to its outer walls, but a sudden thunderstorm put out the fires before it could be totally consumed. It took three years to rebuild the White House, and it wasn't ready to occupancy until after Madison left office in 1817.

"Be always on your guard that you become not the slave of the public, nor the martyr to your friends."
Dolley Madison

After two terms in office, the Madisons retired to the family estate "Montpelier" in Virginia. Madison died in 1836, and financial worries forced Dolley to sell the estate and his papers to pay their debts. Dolley moved back to Washington and became once again the "Grand Dame" of society. She was honored by the House of Representatives with a lifetime seat.

Dolley was a success as a First Lady because she was a good wife, and because she genuinely cared for all people. She treated queens and housemaids just the same.

In spite of her early dismissal from the Society of Friends, she was a lifelong, practicing Christian. She attended church with James, who was an Episcopalian, and frequently wore a large cross. She sent her son to Catholic school. She regularly attended the interdenominational "Sabbaths in the Speaker's Chair," religious services held in Congress. But more than obvious demonstrations of faith, she lived a Christian lifestyle. She became the first directress of an association for orphans, making clothes and raising funds to build the orphanage. Dolley Madison's Quaker piety and genuine concern for others never lessened.

Her only true heartache was her son. He refused to get a job, spent her money, and abandoned her when she needed help. By 1845, when Dolley was in her late seventies (she never told her true age), she sought even more spiritual comfort in the church. For the first time since she left the Quakers 50 years earlier, she joined a church, St. John's Episcopal.

Dolley loved her husband and Washington, and the country loved Dolley Madison. God must have been well pleased.

Lessons From Dolley

Make a joyful noise unto the Lord, all ye lands. Serve the Lord with gladness: come before his presence with singing (Psalm 100:1-2).

Whoso privily slandereth his neighbor, him will I cut off: him that have a high look and a proud heart will not I suffer (Psalm 101:5).

"There is that of God in every man," Although Dolley gave up her membership in the Society of Friends (the Quakers), she kept this fundamental Quaker belief always in her heart. How fortunate the young country was to have Dolley in Washington. She was one of those rare people who truly enjoyed life and wanted everyone around her to enjoy it with the same exuberance that she did. Life wasn't all roses; she lost her husband, her son abandoned her, and she became impoverished, but she drew closer to her faith, never doubting the basic equality and goodness of people.

Dear God, **please help us to remember that life is Your gift to us, that You gave it because You love us and take pleasure when we enjoy and fulfill our purposes. Amen**

5

Elizabeth Kortright Monroe

"La Belle Americaine"

▦ Meet Elizabeth

Born	New York, 1768
Married	James Monroe, 1786
Children	Three (one died in infancy)
First Lady	1817-1825
Died	1830 at age 62
Elizabeth's World	The first public high school opens in Boston; the Unitarian Church is formed; the Erie Canal is completed.

Elizabeth Monroe's one claim to fame came more than 20 years before she entered the White House. While James Monroe was serving as ambassador to France, they learned that Madame Lafayette, a great supporter of the United States, was in prison and about to be executed. Elizabeth took her carriage to the prison and demanded an immediate meeting with Madame Lafayette. Elizabeth announced that she, the ambassador's wife and a very high-profile American representative, would most certainly return for future visits, a bold proclamation that piqued concern among French officials who imprisoned Madame Lafayette. Not wishing to displease Elizabeth (and consequently the American ambassador to France), they released Madame Lafayette one day before she was to have been beheaded.

New Yorker Elizabeth met James Monroe in 1785 and married him within the year. She was only eighteen years old, and he was ten years her senior, but they were in love. Their marriage lasted forty-five years.

Monroe was elected to the United States Senate in 1790 and went to France in 1794 as ambassador. While in Paris, Elizabeth adopted the European styles and formality. When the Monroes

This pier table (left), fruit bsket (center), and candelabrum are some of the elegant items purchased for the White House restoration during the Monroe administration.

returned to the United States and entered the White House in 1817, she brought European culture with her. Her remodeling of the White House after the destruction of the War of 1812 was decried as too ornate and "too French." But there was a bit of wisdom in her decision to re-create an ornamental style. Through her experience as an American ambassador's wife in France, she had learned that European leadership was often royalty. And royalty, accustomed to a measure of finery, regarded the American standard as savage and lowbrow. In replicating opulence, Elizabeth elevated the credibility of the president and his successors in the eyes of European leaders. The president and his wife would never be "king" and "queen," but they would live well and entertain luxuriously in the manner royal.

But all the opulence in the White House could not endear Elizabeth to Washington society, fickle and judgmental. She simply didn't follow the unspoken "rules." First, she refused to make the customary "calls" upon people. And then she further infuriated the upper crust by restricting invitations to their daughter's wedding to only family and a few friends. She was unflatteringly called "Queen Elizabeth." In the kind perspective of history, she was merely a shy, private woman who liked to decorate. And we may now surmise that her biggest problem was following the famous, fabulous Dolley Madison. No one could have.

Elizabeth, although she left an imprint of distinctive style upon the White House, left not a single quote of her own. She was fifty-seven years old when she left the White House. She died suddenly in 1830 at age sixty-two.

Elizabeth belonged to the Episcopal Church and attended church every Sunday. Although faithful in her tithing, almost nothing else is known about her practice in faith. Her daughter, Eliza, converted to Catholicism, but that was not uncommon at the time, especially for young women educated in France. For Elizabeth, pomp and circumstance seemed to be her guiding light.

Lessons from Elizabeth

For where your treasure is, there will your heart be also (Luke 12:34).

Consider the lilies how they grow: they toil not, they spin not; and yet I say unto you Solomon in all of his glory was not arrayed like one of these (Luke 12:27).

Elizabeth lived for the glitter and delighted in the trappings of her position, but she left us little of substance. She was a beautiful woman, and at least once in Paris, she was a courageous woman, but beauty fades and gold darkens. We need to find the substance in life, not the glitter. How often are we drawn by the eye to something that we know is not good or right? The whole industry of "packaging" is to catch our eye so we will buy products because of their appeal, not for their utility. How often are we drawn to people because of their clothes or possessions, or repelled because they lack these things? What a poor measure of a person. Elizabeth may have been a deep, caring person, but we will never know. She left us only glitter.

Dear God, thank You for all that is real. Help us to discern the difference between things that look good and things that are good, and then give us the strength of character to make the right choices. Amen.

6

Louisa Johnson Adams

The White House is "that dull and stately prison in which the sounds of mirth are seldom heard." Louisa Adams

Meet Louisa

Born	England, 1775
Married	John Quincy Adams, 1797
Children	Four (one die in infancy)
First Lady	1825-1829
Died	1852 at age 77
Louisa's World	Webster publishes his *American Dictionary of the Language*; friction matches are introduced; the word "technology" is used for the first time.

Although talented, beautiful, and sophisticated, Louisa could not master one critical job that might have made all the difference between a happy life and one of abject misery: pleasing her mother-in-law, the venerable Abigail Adams. The problem started when her husband John Quincy Adams went against his mother's wishes and married Louisa, a "foreigner." Louisa was born in England to a British mother and an American father, and was educated in France. She was, and is to this day, the only First Lady born outside the United States. While most would see international perspective as a distinct advantage for a First Lady, Abigail Adams was not pleased that her son had selected a woman who had lived under the "wicked" influence of the French.

Louisa did not see the United States until she was 26. She met John Quincy Adams in England in 1795, when he was on a diplomatic mission. They were married three years later. His diplomatic service took them to Berlin, where Louisa displayed all the hospitality, grace, and style of a diplomat's wife ... and showed great promise as a future First Lady.

"Family is and must be secondary to a zealous patriot."
Louisa Adams

In 1801, John and Louisa came to the United States. He served in the Senate. They had three children and lived in Massachusetts until Adams was appointed minister to Russia. They left their two oldest sons with their grandmother in Massachusetts so that they could complete their educations, and moved to St. Petersburg, Russia with their young son. Louisa was not to see her two oldest sons for seven years. Russia was harsh and difficult, and their daughter, born in 1811, died a few months later.

Adams was called back to Paris and wrote to his wife that she needed to close up their residence in St. Petersburg and join him in Paris. So in the beginning of winter, brave Louisa set out with her

Louisa Adams was born, reared, and educated in Europe.

small son and two servants in a Russian carriage across 2,000 miles. The journey took six weeks across war-ravaged Europe, during which they were stranded in the ice, robbed, terrorized and almost taken prisoner by Napoleon's rebels. When they finally arrived in Paris, John, in his usual brash manner, complained that they were late. (He later acquiesced that it had been a remarkable journey.)

They returned to the United States where Adams was appointed Secretary of State under Monroe in 1817 and elected president in 1825.

To say that Louisa disliked the White House is an understatement. Her mother-in-law, Abigail Adams, the second First Lady and wife to President John Adams, knew the demands of the position and doubted that Louisa had sufficient stamina to be her son's helpmate. Perhaps unrelenting judgement and pressure from her mother-in-law were the "straws that broke the camel's back," but Louisa proved her right. Convinced that she was inadequate for her role as First Lady, she spiraled into profound depression. She suffered from migraines and did not participate in any political affairs. She opted for more gentle, undemanding pursuits—growing silk worms, playing her harp, and painting. To relieve the stress of the White House, she sought solace by eating pounds of chocolate. She even attempted to write an autobiography and revealingly entitled it, "Adventures of a Nobody."

In reality, she was a gracious, stylish hostess and a politically astute woman, but was allowed no part in political matters. Had she been allowed, she might have been able to help salvage John's presidency, but he managed alone to alienate his party and refused to seriously campaign for reelection. President John Quincy Adams lost to Andrew Jackson. In 1829, they retired to their home in Quincy, Massachusetts, but for only one year. Adams was elected to the House of Representatives and served successfully until he died of a stroke at work in 1848. Louisa lived four more years in Washington.

Louisa Adams shown winding silk from some of the hundreds of silkworms she raised. Hot water dissolves the gum that cements the cocoon's filiments.

Very little is known about Louisa's faith. She grew up in the Church of England, but was educated in Catholic schools. In her few letters that remain, she reveals a religious and social conscience. When writing to former President Monroe on behalf of her sister, she pleaded, "My religion sanctions it, and I prefer my duty to God to my duty to man." She was loyal to her husband throughout their fifty years of marriage, although their relationship suffered from their long separations and radically different personalities.

John demanded perfection from Louisa and their sons, and found them lacking. Living with him must have been more than challenging. He had no social skills, and alienated people with his shrill voice and cold manner. When their son, George, felt into debt and disrepute, his father sent him scathing letters and insisted that he come to Washington and explain his actions. On the steamboat trip to Washington, George appeared to have had a mental collapse. He committed suicide by jumping overboard. Devastated, Louisa finally saw some humanity and caring in her husband, who evidently reacted to his son's death like a normal, grieving father. They comforted each other by reading Bible passages. At their son's memorial service, John asked Louisa to read the funeral service from the Episcopal Book of Common Prayer.

Their relationship had come full circle in God. John's letters, that a year before had been addressed to "Mrs. Louisa C. Adams," now were penned "Dearest Louisa." Their last years together were their best. Louisa escaped the White House and John Quincy found the success in Congress that had eluded him in the presidency.

Lessons from Louisa

And Ruth said, Intreat me not to leave thee, or to return from following after thee; for whither thou goest, I will go; and

***where thou lodgest, I will lodge: thy people shall be my
people, and thy God my God: Where thou diest, will I die, and
there will I be buried: the Lord do so to me, and more also, if
ought death part thee and me (Ruth 1:16-17).***

The lesson from Louisa is the centuries-old lesson of leaving
our birth families to forge a new family through marriage. The new
family is, of course, a composite of everything that the two people
bring from their parents, but to succeed, it needs to be a new
entity. When copper and tin are merged, they form bronze, a new
substance not like either of their components, but deriving beauty
and strength from both sides. Dominance from either component
ruins the alloy, just as dominance or disdain from either side in a
marriage will destroy the union.

Some of the First Ladies suffered under the glare of their
mothers-in-law, while others rejoiced in the help and assistance
they received. Acceptance is probably the first key—acceptance on
both sides. Marriage is a package deal. People come with
attachments that cannot and should not be completely severed. We
want and need our heritage, our relatives and our traditions, but we
also need to move forward with our own new home and new
traditions. It is a balancing act. Honor thy father and mother. Abide
and comfort thy husband or wife.

And never let a mother-in-law convince you that you're
unworthy.

Dear God, **we truly want to be new people with new
families, but we don't want to change. Please guide and direct
our transformation. We want to be butterflies, but we keep
spinning cocoons, afraid to break out of our mold into a new
life. Please help give us the courage and confidence to
change. Amen.**

7

Rachel Donelson Robards Jackson

*"I would rather be a door-keeper in the house of God
than to live in that palace."*
Rachel Jackson on the White House

Meet Rachel

Born	Virginia, 1767
Married	Lewis Robards, 1784
	Andrew Jackson, 1791, 1794
Children	One adopted son
First Lady	Died just prior to Inauguration
Died	1828 at age 61
Rachel's World	Baltimore and Ohio Railroad begins operation; the Democratic Party is formed.

We know the old children's taunt, "Sticks and stones may break my bones, but words will never hurt me," isn't true and has never been true. For Rachel—survivor of spousal abuse, indian attacks, fever, and hard years on the frontier—words alone proved fatal.

Rachel was born in Virginia, but traveled with her large family to the Tennessee wilderness when she was 13. She married Lewis Robards when she was 17, but the starry-eyed teenaged bride quickly discovered that her new groom had a dark side. He was insanely jealous, unfaithful, and abusive. In fact, he sent her home twice, but always pleaded for her to return to him.

On one trip home to her mother's boarding house, she met the young attorney, Andrew Jackson. Andrew had fierce red hair and a temper to match, and didn't take kindly to anyone who mistreated women, particularly the lovely Rachel. Robards was jealous of Jackson and challenged him to a duel, but backed off.

Robards might have backed off of Andrew Jackson, but Rachel didn't. They were falling in love. After a long separation, Robards filed for divorce, and Rachel and Andrew married. Three years later they discovered that Robards had not finalized the divorce; he had only petitioned to file for one. In fact, to make life for the Jacksons even more miserable, he charged Rachel with bigamy and adultery. The whole matter must have been unsettling to the Jacksons, but they handled it with dignity and in privacy. When the divorce was final, Rachel and Jackson quietly held a second ceremony in 1794 and went on with their lives as though nothing had happened. But the incident would follow them.

Jackson was the first man elected from Tennessee to the House of Representatives. He sat on the Supreme Court of Tennessee. In 1815, he became a became a military hero after a decisive victory at the Battle of New Orleans, where he earned the moniker, "Old Hickory." By 1821, Jackson was named military governor of Florida, and Rachel joined him in Pensacola. It is here that we catch our first glimpse of her faith in action. She described Florida as a wicked, heathen place, and tried to stop music and dancing on the Sabbath.

They returned to their Tennessee home, "The Hermitage," but their respite was cut short when Jackson was elected to the Senate in 1823 and the presidency in 1828.

During the mud-slinging campaigning of the 1828 presidential race, Rachel was libeled and slandered in every possible manner—worse than anything we've seen in media attacks in modern day. Why the intense attacks? The Jacksons' got married before Robards completed divorce proceedings. Scandal! Although Robards was guilty of engineering a deliberately hurtful and embarrassing situation to exact revenge on Rachel and Jackson, no one thought to place blame where blame was due. Although the Jacksons were innocent of wrongdoing, and the painful mistake in timing had been quickly, legally remedied, Rachel alone took the full brunt of Robards' evil plot. She was labeled "uncouth," an "adulteress," and a "Jezebel." Jackson tried to shield her from the worst of the attacks and fought several duels to protect her honor, but he could not stop the press or gossipmongers who delighted in the buzz of righteous indignation and puritanical judgement. On a shopping trip to Nashville to buy her inaugural gown, Rachel overheard some women talking about her and how someone so sinful could not possibly live in the White House. Rachel collapsed and had to be carried home. She died of a heart attack just days later.

Rachel had been an unsophisticated child of the frontier. Although she knew how to read and write, she had little formal schooling. She never had children, but surrounded herself with nieces and nephews. In fact, she and Jackson adopted one nephew as their own son. His name was Andrew Jackson Donelson. He married his cousin, Emily. It was she who served as President Jackson's First Lady in the White House after Rachel died.

We know that Rachel was a woman of extraordinary faith. Rachel's religion grew as she grew. She became a devout Presbyterian, and church became her only activity outside of her family and friends. While in Washington, Rachel was impressed with the number of churches and the quality of the preaching, so she felt at home there. She always traveled with her Bible, and attended Sunday church and Thursday prayer meetings wherever she was.

We also know that she was an activist in the name of the Lord. While in New Orleans with her "General," Rachel requested military help to restore order by closing the gambling houses.

However noble and admirable her piety, it also increased her guilt to the point that the stress of it probably killed her. She felt that God was punishing her for her "former sins." At her funeral, with his wife lying in repose in her inaugural gown, Jackson once again displayed his fiery temperament by raising his cane to heaven and declaring through tears of bitterness, "In the presence of this dead saint I can and do forgive all my enemies. But those vile wretches who have slandered her must look to God for mercy."

Lessons from Rachel

But I say unto you, that every idle word that men shall speak, they shall give account thereof in the day of judgment (Matthew 12:36).

Reproach hath broken my heart; and I am full of heaviness: and I looked for some to take pity, but there was none (Psalm 69:20).

From Rachel we learn two hard lessons: we can never escape our past, and we need strength to withstand the cruel words and actions that inevitably come our way. Life wasn't fair to Rachel. She didn't deserve the abuse or the perception of scandal. Her mistake was in focusing on what other people thought. Worse, Rachel focused on her perceived sin instead of on our guaranteed forgiveness. Her God was a punishing God, and poor Rachel couldn't stand up to the anticipation of punishment. What a different story it would have been if she had been able to hold her head high and march into the White House and prove all her critics wrong. We aren't here to be judged by other people. We are judged only by God. Rachel forgot that. God gives us strength to do such brave things, but first we have to ask.

Dear God, uncover our strengths. Deep down inside we know You will never give us more than we can handle, but sometimes our doubts, sins, and guilt pile up on our strengths and we forget or deny that they exist. Help us establish a daily workout for our faith. With repetitions and a routine, we will uncover strengths to meet any challenge. Amen.

8

Hannah Hoes Van Buren

"She was an ornament of the Christian Faith."

 ## Meet Hannah

Born	New York, 1783
Married	Martin Van Buren, 1807
Children	Five (one died in infancy)
First Lady	Died prior to husband's election
Died	1819 at age 35
Hannah's World	Spain cedes Florida to the United States; the Unitarian Church is formed.

*O*ld Kinderhook was a very small, very Dutch town known for two things: It's the birthplace of President Martin Van Buren, and it's also the birthplace of our almost universal expression "OK." How the initials for Old Kinderhook became synonymous for "all right" is unknown or at least has nothing to do with Hannah Van Buren and her faith.

Hannah Hoes was born in Kinderhook of Dutch parents. She grew up speaking Dutch and playing with her neighbor, "Matty" Van Buren. (He called her Jannetje, in the Dutch language of their families.) Martin became a successful lawyer and made sure that his law practice was firmly established before he took Hannah for his wife when they were both 24. They moved to Hudson and then to Albany as Martin entered politics and became a state senator and state attorney general. Historians have concluded that their marriage was a short, but happy one. They had, after all, been childhood sweethearts.

Hannah had four sons in ten years. She died shortly after the birth of her fourth son at the age of 35, after a prolonged illness, probably tuberculosis.

Virtually nothing is known about Hannah, but two surviving, commissioned portraits portray her as being stunningly beautiful and delicate. Van Buren did not remarry after her death, so we might conclude that he loved her too much to consider replacing her, but he never mentioned her in his autobiography. She left no written correspondence, so personal glimpses into her life do not exist. What little we do know is that Hannah was pious and devoted woman. She grew up in the Dutch Reformed Church. When the Van Burens moved to Hudson, she joined the First Presbyterian Church, because there was no Dutch Reformed Church in town. She was also active in the Second Presbyterian Church in Albany when they moved there in 1817. The church was known for its progressive programs, including a Sunday School to teach the orphans of the streets how to read and write.

Angelica Singleton Van Buren

Knowing that she was about to die, Hannah called her children to her and "committed them to the care of the Savior she loved." She also instructed her husband not to spend money on a funeral, but to give the funds to the poor.

It would be eighteen years before her husband and four handsome, grown sons entered the White House, but she would have been very proud of them. As they moved in, none other than the "Grand Dame" of Washington, Dolley Madison, was watching the parade. She knew that five men on their own could not manage the mansion. Using her best matchmaking skills, she invited her beautiful cousin, Angelica Singleton, up from South Carolina for a visit, and they went calling at the White House. In less than a year, Angelica married the oldest Van Buren son, and took over the role of First Lady, becoming a gracious and charming White House hostess.

Lessons from Hannah

And now abideth faith, hope, charity, these three, but the greatest of these is charity (1 Corinthians 13:13).

We know almost nothing about the life of Hannah Van Buren, but the one account we have of her on her deathbed reveals almost all we need to know about this dear lady. She was only 35, dying, and leaving a beloved husband and four beloved children, yet she said nothing about herself. In her final hours, she worried about her children and wanted to be sure God kept close watch on them. She worried about her charities. She didn't want any money spent on her funeral; she wanted the money spent on the poor. Her niece Maria said that Hannah's deathbed farewell was made in "perfect composure." Hannah certainly had faith, hope, and charity. Faith in her Savior, hope for her family, and charity for the world. What a beautiful, selfless person.

Dear God, may we be blessed with the faith, hope and charity of Hannah Van Buren, to always look first to the needs of others, no matter what our personal positions. May we be the ones to toss the life preservers, knowing that our faith is pure and our own salvation is not in our hands, but Yours. Amen.

9

Anna Tuthill Symmes Harrison

"Every public and private charity was near her heart."

Meet Anna

Born	New Jersey, 1775
Married	William Henry Harrison, 1795
Children	10 (only two outlived her)
First Lady	1841
Died	1864 at age 88
Anna's World	Indian Wars rage in the frontier; the Smithsonian opens in Washington; Massachusetts rules that children under 12 cannot work more than a 10-hour day.

Anna Harrison was a First Lady with several "firsts." She was the first presidential wife from the frontier and the first with a formal education. But in spite of credentials that would have made her interesting and effective as a First Lady, we'll never know what pages she would have written in the history books. She never made it to the White House. When her husband, William Henry Harrison, was inaugurated in 1841, Anna was too ill to travel in winter and remained at their home in Ohio. President Harrison presented the longest inaugural speech in history, caught pneumonia in the freezing weather, and died after just one month in office. Perhaps if Anna had been present, she would have convinced him to shorten his speech or cover his head.

Anna lived for another 22 years in Ohio.

Anna was born and raised in New Jersey, but her father moved the family to a new settlement in North Bend, Ohio (at that time, still the "frontier"). It was there that she met young military officer, William Harrison. Her father objected to Harrison, saying he was a man, "who can neither bleed (as a doctor), plead (as a lawyer) nor preach, and if he could plow I would be satisfied." That didn't dissuade Anna, who waited until her father was away on a trip and married Harrison in front of a justice of the peace when she was twenty years old. Anna followed her husband all over the new country in his military career until their family became too large, and they returned to settle in North Bend.

Harrison was governor of the Indiana Territory for 12 years and during that time fought the famous Indian Chief, Tecumseh, in a battle near Tippecanoe Creek. It was not an important battle, but Harrison went on to become a brigadier general in the War of 1812, and effectively destroyed the alliance that the Indians had formed with the British. After the war, Harrison served in the House of Representatives and the Senate. When the Whigs needed a famous name to run against Van Buren for president, they remembered the war hero, Harrison, and nicknamed him "Tippecanoe." His vice-presidential candidate was John Tyler, so "Tippecanoe and Tyler, too" became a very successful campaign slogan—certainly one of the most famous in American history.

At age 65, after a lifetime of military service with frequent moves and long separations, Anna had looked forward to retirement, not a new career. When her husband was nominated for president, Anna was, to say the least, dismayed. Running the country was a far cry from the leisurely life of a retired gentleman farmer and his wife. When Harrison left in February for the inauguration, Anna was ill and still distraught over the recent death of a son. She promised to join her husband in the White House in the spring but she never left Ohio. Harrison was inaugurated on March 4, 1841and died on April 4, 1841.

With her husband in the military, Anna was frequently alone on the frontier, managing the farm and rearing ten children. She set up a school in her home and hired a tutor for her children and others in the community.

Anna was a devout Presbyterian and remained deeply religious throughout her life. When Harrison was territorial governor of Indiana, she insisted that no official business be conducted on Sunday, honoring God's instruction for a day of rest. Church was always the highlight of her week, and she was well known for inviting the whole congregation to their home for Sunday dinner. She continued her "Sunday feasts" for years, with as many as fifty hungry guests at her table at one time.

At no time was her faith more evident than during the seven years in which she lost her beloved William and six of her seven children. Anna persevered through unshakable faith, turning more and more to her Bible and her church.

She died in 1864 in the home of her only surviving son, John. Also raised in that home was her grandson, Benjamin. Benjamin was fighting in the Civil War at the time of her death, but he would return to become the 23rd president of the United States, thus continuing his grandparents' traditions of leadership, courage, and devotion to God.

Lessons from Anna

And I will bless her, and give thee a son also of her: yea, I will bless her, and she shall be a mother of nations; kings of people shall be of her. Then Abraham fell upon his face and laughed, and said in his heart, Shall a child be born unto him that is a hundred years old? And shall Sarah, that is ninety years old, bear? (Genesis 17:16-17)

Anna Harrison surely read the story of Sarah and Abraham in the Bible, and took it to heart. At age 65, she was *ready* to move to Washington and take over as First Lady for her husband—a whole new career in a new home in a new city. We are never too old for God to use our talents. We need to banish the word "retirement" from our vocabulary and speak instead of "replenish" and "recycle." What wondrous opportunities await us when we finish our first careers! Look at the truly gifted and creative people of the ages, and you will find that many did not even start on their "life's work" until their 60s or 70s or later! Grandma Moses didn't even start painting until she was 79 and illustrated her first book when she was 100! It is never too late or too difficult with God's help.

Dear God, thank You for making me just the way I am so that I may further Your kingdom on earth. My pace may slow and my eyes may dim, but there is always work to be done, and Your work will keep me young. Amen.

10 a

Letitia Christian Tyler

"The most entirely unselfish person you can imagine."
Priscilla Cooper Tyler, Letitia's daughter-in-law, wife to Robert

Meet Letitia

Born	Virginia, 1790
Married	John Tyler, 1813
Children	Nine (two died in infancy)
First Lady	1841-1842
Died	1842 at age 51
Letitia's World	United States-Canada border established; *New York Tribune* starts publication.

Letitia Tyler suffered a stroke in 1839 and never fully recovered. She was confined to a wheelchair and spent much of her time confined to her room. When her husband, John Tyler, took oath as Vice President in the administration of President William Henry Harrison, he fully expected to be able to dispatch most of his duties from their plantation in Williamsburg, Virginia so that he could keep Letitia at home. But life has a way of taking unexpected turns. When President Harrison died one month into office, Vice President Tyler became the first man to become president due to the death of the sitting president. He was dubbed, "His Accidency." Probably no one was more acutely aware of the accidental commitment that had been made than Letitia. Staying at home in the comfort of Virginia was suddenly no longer an option. Letitia was First Lady, like it or not.

Letitia Christian was born on a wealthy Tidewater Virginia plantation in 1790 and rarely left Virginia for the next fifty years. She was courted by John Tyler for five years before her parents gave their blessing. Although only 23 at the time, John was already a member of the Virginia House of Delegates. At 26, he was Congressman, and at 35, was governor of Virginia. Letitia had no formal education except what she was taught at home, but that did not hinder her in managing a series of plantations, raising seven children, and keeping the family solvent while her husband pursued his political career. Only once did she join him in Washington for the social season.

When her husband was thrust into the role of president of the United States, Letitia gallantly followed her husband to the White House. Even though she was firmly affixed in family life, she rarely left her room on the second floor. Her only public appearance was the wedding of her daughter in January 1842. She is described by her daughter-in-law Priscilla as "surpassingly lovely" and greeting her guests "in her sweet, gentle, self-possessed manner." We know Letitia through Priscilla's notes, for none of Letitia's letters survived and she managed to stay always in the background.

In September 1842, Letitia suffered another stroke and died the next day with a damask rose in her hand. She was the first president's wife to die in the White House. Her daughter-in-law Priscilla and daughter Elizabeth (with some outside advice from none other than Dolley Madison) served as White House hostesses for the next two years.

For Letitia, her religion was her life. She taught her children their letters by using the Bible. After her stroke in 1839, the only books she read were her Bible and her prayer book. The biographer, Mary Whitton, states, "There was no lip service in Letitia Tyler's religion. She accepted the theology of her church as unquestioningly as she accepted all of the other standards of her time. But her piety came from the heart." Priscilla said, "She had everything about her to awaken love."

Lessons from Letitia

Yea, though I walk through the valley of the shadow of death, I will fear no evil: for thou are with me; thy rod and thy staff they comfort me (Psalm 23:4).

From Letitia we learn the lesson of abiding in faith. Letitia was only 50 when she entered the White House, but she entered in a wheelchair. Even though she was unable to participate in most of the activities of the house, she was described by her daughter-in-law as the most gentle, refined, and unselfish person she had ever met. Letitia accepted her position; did not begrudge other people their health or abilities; and maintained a solid faith that inspired all who met her. After raising seven children and surviving more than 25 years as the wife of a politician, perhaps Letitia was ready for another life. As her faith was sure, she had no fear.

Dear God, thank You for memories and for dreams. We know that no matter how bad our present situation may seem, we can experience happiness in an instant by remembering all of the beautiful people and events in our past, and anticipating all of the beautiful people and events yet to come. Amen.

10 b

Julia Gardiner Tyler

"The Lady Presidentress"

▣ *Meet Julia*

Born	New York, 1820
Married	John Tyler, 1844
Children	Seven
First Lady	1844-1845
Died	1889 at age 69
Julia's World	First telegraph message sent; United States Naval Academy opens; Territory of Texas annexed.

Julia was President John Tyler's second wife. She is described as being the complete opposite of his first wife, Letitia. "The Rose of Long Island" was a formally educated, beautiful, society girl from a wealthy New York family. But she had embarrassed her family at the age 19 by posing for a department store advertisement. Proper ladies did not have their names or pictures in the news, and she was promptly sent to Europe for a long tour until the scandal abated.

Julia had many admirers, including the widower Tyler. She refused Tyler's first proposal of marriage, but changed her mind after her father was killed in a tragic explosion aboard a Navy ship. John comforted her and won her heart. She was only 24 when she covertly married John Tyler, a 54-year-old widow with seven children. Tyler was the first president to marry in office. Public comments on the secret wedding ranged from "Lucky Honest John" to "poor, unfortunate, deluded old jackass." Relations with her new stepchildren were problematic ... especially since three of them were older than she was at the time of her marriage. Undaunted and undeterred, Julia was an energetic and devoted spouse and had seven children with Tyler before his death in 1862 at 71. John fathered his last child with Julia at the age of 70.

Julia only served eight months as First Lady, but she loved her role and the White House. She didn't just entertain at the White House; she "reigned." She established her own court and was the first First Lady to have a press agent. She also instituted the custom of the Marine Band playing "Hail to the Chief," and introduced the polka in the White House. She increased Tyler's popularity ... and his jealousy. She loved parties, politics and flirting, She had a pet Italian Greyhound and exited the White House with an extravagant ball for over 3,000 attendees.

After leaving the White House, the Tylers settled in his new plantation, "Sherwood Forest" in Virginia. Although born in New York, Julia adopted Southern culture and customs. Both John and

In 1844, Julia Gardiner Tyler was the first First Lady to be photographed.

Julia became supporters of state's rights, and John became the only ex-president to hold office in the Confederacy. Their sons and grandsons served in the Confederacy. John died in 1862, and Julia had to abandon Sherwood Forest during the Civil War and seek refuge in New York. The Civil War not only destroyed her home, but caused severe financial problems for her until she received an income from her mother's estate in 1873. Congress also awarded her a widow's pension in 1882.

Although a participating Episcopalian most of her life, Julia converted to the Roman Catholic faith in the 1870s. Her youngest daughter attended a convent school. Her support of the Confederacy also became a religious crusade. "The hand of Providence should assist this holy cause," she proclaimed in an attempt to enlist volunteers. Julia died in Richmond in 1889 in the same hotel where her beloved John died 27 years before.

Lessons from Julia

Live joyfully with the wife whom thy lovest all the days of the life of thy vanity, which he hath given thee under the sun (Ecclesiastes 9:9).

Psychologists looking at the story of Julia would be quick to point out that she paid little attention to "that old man Tyler" until her father was killed, and that then she was surely drawn to Tyler because he was a father figure more than a husband. Perhaps, but it worked. This was one of several May-December marriages of the First Families ... and they all thrived. Julia brought great ceremony and celebration to the White House and even excitement with "lucky John" chasing her around the East Room for a kiss. She not only bore Tyler another seven children, but she returned with him to Virginia after the White House and became his soul mate in their fight for the Confederacy in the Civil War. Age didn't matter. On his sixty-second birthday, she composed a poem in which she declared, "What e'er changes time may bring, I'll love thee as thou art!" Our lesson from Julia? Those whom God hath joined together, let no man put asunder. Neither should we second guess.

Dear God, **save us from our own self-righteousness. Even though we are sure we know what is right for our neighbors, our relatives, and their children, direct us to work on ourselves, not others. Thank You for Your help, with which we will be better people. Amen.**

11

Sarah Childress Polk

*"I recognize nothing in myself;
I am only an atom in the hands of God."* Sarah Polk

Meet Sarah

Born	Tennessee, 1803
Married	James K. Polk, 1824
Children	None
First Lady	1845-1849
Died	1891 at age 87
Sarah's World	United States at war with Mexico over the annexation of Texas; first recorded baseball game is played in New Jersey; Stephen Foster writes *Oh Susanna!*

Sarah Polk was considered the perfect wife for a young politician. She was wealthy, intelligent and good-looking. She had the benefit of having been educated at the Moravians' "female academy" in North Carolina, one of the few institutions of higher learning for women at that time. She was also an avid reader and interested in politics. And she was ambitious. In fact, supposedly she agreed to marry James Polk only if he won a seat in the Tennessee legislature. He did and they married in 1824. Sarah was a true helpmate. Not only did she run their home, but she actively participated in his campaigns for the United States Congress and for governor of Tennessee. During their 14 years in Washington, while Polk was a Congressman, Sarah functiond as his private secretary and quiet advisor while also serving as a charming and gracious hostess. When James Polk was elected president in 1845, Sarah continued as his closest and most trusted advisor.

Sarah and James were described as the hardest working couple in the White House. Since they had no children, they worked together twelve hours a day and never took a vacation. In their entire four-year administration, they were only away from the

James Polk, center left, Sarah, center right.

White House three days. Their goals were to expand the United States to the Rio Grande, to the Pacific and to Canada. They accomplished all of them, adding more than 800,000 square miles of territory to the country.

They did entertain and had twice-weekly receptions, but there was no entertainment and no refreshments were served. Although prim, Sarah was also popular and a formidable politician. When Polk's opponent's wife, Mrs. Henry Clay, claimed to be a model wife because she knew how to make good butter and keep a spotless house, Sarah announced that with the president's salary she would have need to "neither keep house nor make butter."

Sarah was born into a wealthy planter family and educated in the best schools in Tennessee and North Carolina. Her family was strict Calvinist, and her religion was a central part of her life that remained in tact through her adult years. When the Polks entered the White House in 1845, she stopped dances. In fact, she attended the Presidential Inaugural Ball, but refused to dance. They also did not attend any theater, concerts, races, or card parties. Some historians conjecture that the Polks never served wine at state dinners, but a Congressman's wife's diary details a four-hour dinner during which six different wines were served. Perhaps the Polks didn't imbibe themselves, but provided for their guests. We do know for certain that Sarah refused to conduct any business or formal entertainment on Sundays. She and the president attended First Presbyterian Church every Sunday, and if any visitors appeared on Sunday morning at the White House, they were swept along to church.

> *"The greater the prosperity, the deeper the sense of gratitude to the Almighty."*
> Sarah Polk

President Polk declined a second term and they retired to their Nashville mansion, "Polk Place." Polk became ill shortly after retiring and died just three months after leaving the White House. Sarah Polk was only 46 and lived another 42 years. She was a good manager and not only kept the Nashville home flourishing, but also oversaw operation of their Mississippi plantation until she sold it in 1860. Although from the South, Sarah kept Polk Place as a neutral site during the Civil War and entertained both Union and

Confederate officers. She stayed at Polk Place until her death in 1891, never leaving except to go to church. For Sarah, religion was her life, and this life was simply a preparation for the next and greater life in heaven.

Lessons from Sarah

And on the seventh day God ended his work which he had made, and he rested on the seventh day from all his work which he had made (Genesis 2:2-3).

If thou turn away thy foot from the sabbath, from doing thy pleasure on my holy day; and call the sabbath a delight, the holy of the Lord; honorable; Then shalt thou delight thyself in the Lord (Isaiah 58 13-14).

Sarah was a puritan and a politician—a rare combination indeed. She knew her place as a traditional wife, and yet was a true partner with her husband throughout his political career. If they had lived in the 21st century, Sarah would have probably been the political office holder instead of her husband. Within the confines of her own time, she had to compromise her own ambitions to those of her husband. But in the practice of her religion, there was no compromise. Since she did not believe in dancing, at the Inaugural Ball all dancing ceased when the presidential couple entered the ballroom and didn't start up again until they left. Once while campaigning, they were on a boat that docked at a town on a Sunday afternoon. A local band started playing as they exited the boat. Sarah refused to leave the boat until the band stopped playing, because it was the Sabbath and she abideth no entertainment on Sunday. No compromise, no matter how appalled other people might have been.

It is hard to tell if Sarah had a happy life. She had a successful life and certainly maintained her principles wherever she went. She had no children, so she was able to work beside her husband everyday of their married life, except, of course, on Sundays. They never took a vacation. Sarah survived the heavy workload, but James did not. We have to admire Sarah for her principles, her steadfastness, and her constancy. It didn't matter whether she was in the greatest house in the country, on a boat, or on a farm, Sunday was the Lord's day. Period.

Dear God, **thank You for the Sabbath. We all need rest and replenishment. Remind us to take this day of rest, no matter how busy we are and how tempted to use this day to catch up or get ahead, so that we will be strengthened. Help us to find our rest in You. Amen.**

12

Margaret Mackall Smith Taylor

"A most reluctant First Lady"

Betty Taylor Bliss, Margaret's daughter,
served as hostess in her mother's place.

 ## Meet Margaret

Born	Maryland, 1788
Married	Zachary Taylor, 1810
Children	Six (two died in infancy)
First Lady	1849-1850
Died	1852 at age 63
Margaret's World	California becomes a state; Hawthorne publishes *The Scarlet Letter*; the safety pin is invented.

Margaret Taylor was so withdrawn and private that no photograph or portrait exists of her. She missed her husband's presidential inauguration by pleading ill health, and when she later arrived in Washington, she remained out of the public eye. When her husband, President Zachary Taylor, died suddenly only 16 months into his presidential term, many didn't even know that he was married or that Margaret actually lived in the White House.

Why the cloak and dagger act? Margaret had promised God during the Mexican War that if General Taylor returned safely, she would never go into society again. He returned. She dropped out of sight.

It was a shame, actually, because Margaret Taylor was born to be a First Lady, with all the training and social skills gleaned from growing up in a prosperous Maryland family and attending finishing school in New York. When her father died, her older sister married and moved to the frontier region of Kentucky. It was there on a visit that Margaret met the young Army Lieutenant Zachary Taylor. She married him in 1810 and spent most of the next 40 years following him from outpost to outpost. The Taylors lived in the territories and forts of Indiana, Illinois, Minnesota, and Louisiana. They survived Indian attacks and malaria.

Zachary resigned his commission in 1814 and started farming, but he was called back by President Madison in 1816 to take command of a fort in Wisconsin. After two hard winters, the Taylors were assigned to Mississippi and Louisiana. Margaret and her two youngest children became very ill, and both children died in less than four months. The family moved back north to Michigan to Fort Crawford, where Taylor started a Temperance Society, library and school. Finally in 1840, after thirty years of marriage and moving, they were assigned back to Baton Rouge and moved into their first permanent home. Margaret loved her little cottage and was determined to plant vegetables, watch the river flow lazily by, and live in peace with her husband. But the government had other ideas. Taylor was a popular war hero, and a new war was brewing. General Taylor was ordered into action by President Polk, and "Old Rough and Ready" commanded impressive victories in the Seminole and Mexican Wars.

Of their three surviving daughters, all three married military men, two of them against the parents' wishes. Their middle daughter, Sarah Knox eloped with the young Jefferson Davis, but died of malaria just three months after the marriage. Taylor refused to speak with Davis for over nine years. Jefferson Davis redeemed himself by resigning from Congress and fighting with Taylor in the Mexican War. Davis remarried, but remained close to the Taylor family.

By 1848, Margaret was sixty and wanted only to retire in Baton Rouge. When Zachary was nominated as president of the United States, she prayed that he wouldn't be elected. When he won the election, she claimed it was a plot to shorten his life and deprive her of his company. She reluctantly came to Washington, but stayed in the private quarters of the White House and rarely attended any social functions. Her youngest daughter, Betty served as the White House hostess. The White House, not a happy place for Margaret anyway, soon turned tragic. The president collapsed as he laid the cornerstone for the Washington Monument on a very hot July Fourth in 1850. He died shortly thereafter. Margaret's greatest fear had been realized. Her dear companion had survived forty years of military service, long winters, Indian attacks, fever and famine, but the duties of the White House proved fatal. Margaret went to live with her son in Mississippi, but her heart and her will were broken. She died two years later.

Although little is known about this dutiful military wife, what little is known reveals a very religious woman. Margaret was a devout Episcopalian; even though she was in fragile health while in the White House, she always attended church services. While serving in military outposts in Minnesota and Louisiana, the Taylors established post chapels. Margaret requested that the services be read from the Episcopal prayer book. One appearance she did make in the White House was to greet a Baptist Sunday school group. In fact, she accepted life membership in the American Sunday School Union. Margaret's heart was with God and her family. Her heart never made it to Washington.

Lessons from Margaret

The Lord is my light and my salvation; whom shall I fear? The Lord is the strength of my life; of whom shall I be afraid? (Psalm 27: 1)

Though a host should encamp against me, my heart shall not fear: though war should rise against me, in this will I be confident (Psalm 27:3).

Upon this rock I will build my church; and the gates of hell shall not prevail against it (Matthew 16:18).

What adjustments Margaret had to make in her life! She went from a wealthy Maryland home, to a private finishing school, and then to the isolated forts and rough cabins of the frontier. Did she even know how to do the laundry? Her life sounds like Moses "wandering in the wilderness for 40 years." And then her life came full circle as she found herself back in the East and in a mansion.

Her faith and her love must have been profound. Even her own illness and the death of two children didn't cause her to waiver or forsake her Lord. She was as much a "rock" as her husband, her "Rough and Ready" war hero ... perhaps even more so. He had an army to defend and accompany him, while Margaret was frequently alone with only a few disabled soldiers and the other wives and children against the elements and enemies of the frontier.

From Margaret we learn love, faith, courage, and adaptability. She followed her husband all over the new country from Minnesota in the winter to the White House in the spring. When he passed away, she felt her job on earth was complete and she was ready to accompany him to yet their next destination.

Dear God, thank You for the adventures of our lives when we turn all the control over to You. Help us to remember that You are always with us to guide us and keep us safe until You lead us home. Amen.

13

Abigail Powers Fillmore

"A lady of great strength of mind"

🔲 Meet Abigail

Born	New York, 1798
Married	Millard Fillmore, 1826
Children	Two (one son, one daughter)
First Lady	1850-1853
Died	1853 at age 55
Abigail's World	The United States population is about 23 million, including over 3 million slaves; Congress reduces postage rates to three cents; Harriet Beecher Stowe publishes *Uncle Tom's Cabin*.

Abigail looked over her new class of students and jumped when she saw the "new boy" in the back. He was a tall 18-year old by the name of Millard Fillmore. It was 1818, and Abigail herself was only 20, but she had been teaching school for four years. She didn't mind an older student ... as long as he really wanted to learn. Millard was probably 10 years older than most of the other students, but he desperately wanted to learn to read and write and become a lawyer. That was an ambitious dream for a poor farm boy who had earned his own way chopping wood since he was 12.

Abigail knew what it meant to be poor. She was the daughter of a Baptist preacher who died when she was only two. Her mother moved further west in New York, hoping for a place to live where their meager funds would go further. Slightly "schooled" and largely educated by her mother with books from her father's library, Abigail started teaching school when she was 16. She also started the first lending library in the small town of Sempronius.

Although Millard wanted to marry her shortly after they met, they waited for over seven years. He worked in a sawmill while studying to be a lawyer and built a house by his own hands for his new bride. They married in 1826 in her brother's house. Even though married, Abigail continued as a schoolteacher, a most unusual situation for the early 1800s. She continued to work until she gave birth to their only son, Millard Powers, born in 1828. Their daughter was born in 1832, after the family had returned to Buffalo, New York, to enjoy the prosperity of Millard's thriving practice.

Millard was elected to the State Assembly, then to Congress. In 1851 he was selected as Zachary Taylor's running mate and elected vice-president. When President Taylor died after only 16 months in office (the second president to die in office), Millard Fillmore took over. Abigail, the former school marm, was suddenly the First Lady.

Ever the schoolteacher, Abigail kept on reading and learning throughout her life. She taught herself French and music. Earlier as the wife of Congressman Fillmore and later as the wife of the president, she actively participated in political discussions. She and Millard never forgot the hard life of the working class, from which they had come, and worked to improve working conditions. Millard abolished flogging and rum in the Navy. The sailors were sure to approve of the first, if not the second change. Abigail had the first bathtub installed in the White House, so the servants didn't have to carry water by hand. They had the first iron cooking range to take some of the drudge out of kitchen work, but no one knew how to use it (Fillmore had to write to the manufacturer for instructions).

They also decided to bring culture to the White House. Abigail broke with social protocol by attending a concert outside the White House, a concert by none other than Jenny Lind. Also, Abigail was appalled that there was not one book in the White House, not even a Bible or dictionary, and quickly started the first White House Library.

Abigail always kept the Sabbath and closed the White House on Sundays for purposes of both rest and religion. The Fillmores were "equal opportunity Christians." She was a Baptist, Millard was a Methodist, and they were married by an Episcopalian. Later they joined the Unitarian Church in Buffalo and attended every Sunday.

Fillmore was not reelected, but his greatest loss came just after they left the White House. Their belongings were all packed and already at the Willard Hotel prior to Inauguration Day. They were planning to leave on a yearlong trip to Europe. Out of deference to incoming President Pierce and his wife, who had just lost their only son in a train accident, Abigail stayed in Washington and attended all of the outdoor inauguration ceremonies for the new president. It was a bitterly cold first of March, and Abigail caught a chill, which quickly developed into pneumonia. She died three weeks later without ever leaving Washington.

Lessons from Abigail

And thou shall teach my people the difference between the holy and the profane, and cause them to discern between the unclean and the clean (Ezekiel 44:23).

Boast not thyself of tomorrow; for thou knowest not what a day may bring forth (Proverbs 27:1).

Whereas ye know not what shall be on the morrow. For what is your life? It is even a vapor, that appeareth for a little time, and then vanisheth away (James 4:14).

From Abigail we learn three strong lessons; the value of teaching and books, remembering where we come from, and the unpredictability of life. Abigail was first a teacher, and even though she gave up her career, she never stopped teaching. She valued education and built the first White House Library to impart that value to all of the First Families to come. She also remembered her days of poverty and hard work, and did not forget the hardships when she entered the White House. She put in laborsaving devices for the benefit of the servants, not for her own convenience. And last, we learn to not postpone joy. The Fillmores were going on their first real vacation and their bags were packed when Abigail fell ill and died. How many people work all of their lives so that they can retire and go on the trip of their dreams, only to have their dreams end, before the joy begins? Take time now to see the beauties that God has made. We know not what tomorrow brings.

Dear God, help us to be open notebooks, ready to be filled with knowledge and directions from those who came before us, and who surround us every day. Keep us receptive to change and not stuck in our recliners. Amen.

14

Jane Means Appleton Pierce

"The shadow in the White House"

▨ *Meet Jane*

Born	New Hampshire, 1806
Married	Franklin Pierce, 1834
Children	Three sons (one died in infancy, one at age 4, and one at age 11)
First Lady	1853-1857
Died	1863 at age 57
Jane's World	Religious revival sweeps across the country; bitter debates and fights occur in Congress over the slavery issue; condensed milk and a pencil with an attached eraser are patented.

Life for Jane Pierce, First Lady to President Franklin Pierce, started out as gray and turned into black.

Jane Pierce was always a frail, delicate woman, given to melancholy and introspection. She was the daughter of a Congregational minister who became president of Bowdoin College. However, her father literally worked, prayed, and fasted himself to death, leaving a widow and six children. Franklin Pierce was a student at Bowdoin and met young Jane there. They married six years later, when Franklin was already involved in politics as a Representative from New Hampshire. Jane was 28—practically "old" in the standards of her day in which brides were almost always much younger. An unlikely pair, Franklin was hearty and outgoing, she shy and aloof. He loved politics, she thought it evil. He loved to drink, she abstained. He loved crowds and parties, she preferred quiet dinners at home. It must be true that opposites attract, because somehow they managed almost thirty years of marriage, but not without much grief and tragedy.

Their first son died after only three days. They had two more sons, but the older son died when he was four years old of typhus fever. That left only little Benny, who became his mother's obsession.

The Pierce family lived in Concord and joined the Congregational Church while Pierce served in Congress. Jane did not like Washington and wanted Franklin to retire from politics. He did for a short time, but his love for politics would soon take him to the pinnacle. When he was nominated for president in 1852, Jane fainted. When Franklin convinced her that his being president would be an asset to Benny's future success, she finally agreed to move to Washington. But on the train trip to the Capitol, there was a train wreck and dear Benny was killed right before their eyes. The nation shared their grief. The Inaugural Ball was cancelled, and Jane did not come to Washington for nearly a month to join her husband. Grieving Jane retreated to a state of severe depression from which she never recovered. She lived in the White House, but made no public appearances for almost two years.

After the Pierces left the White House, they traveled in search of health cures for Jane, but were never successful. She died of tuberculosis six years after leaving the White House.

Jane was born and raised in a devoutly religious family and brought the same piety into her own family. She insisted on family worship every morning, prayers every evening and church every Sunday. She instructed Benny daily with Bible stories and

Correspondence between Jane Pierce and her sister Mary Aiken and her family was published by a private collector and donated to the Library of the First Ladies.

hymns. However, Jane never found happiness. She blamed Franklin for the death of their son; it was because of his political ambitions that they and Benny were on that ill-fated train. Franklin, also plagued with grief and guilt, was unable to provide any effective leadership during his one term of office. Although they traveled after leaving the White House, hoping that a change of climate would improve Jane's health, nothing helped. Wherever she went, she carried her beloved Benny's Bible with her. Jane believed that God was punishing them and remained despondent until her death from tuberculosis six years after leaving the White House. Nathaniel Hawthorne, a colleague and close friend of Franklin, noted at her funeral service that she had never had anything to do with "things present." She focused on the spiritual all of her life, but sadly, never found joy in the spirit.

Lessons from Jane

I am weary of my crying; my throat is dried: mine eyes fail while I wait for my God (Psalm 69:3).

For thou are my hiding place; thou shalt preserve me from trouble (Psalm 33:7).

Thou are my hiding place and my shield: I hope in thy word (Psalm 119:114).

Jane never learned joy. She grew up in a home where her father felt personally responsible for the souls of all of his students, and prayed for them sometimes all night long. Her childhood was the perfect breeding ground for depression. Jane was a beautiful woman and wanted to be a warm and caring wife and mother, but she didn't know how to even start. Her losses would have been hard on a strong person, but for Jane death came years before she ceased breathing. Help was there, right in the same book she read every day. But Jane must have read only Job or perhaps the Psalms of anguish, but never the twenty-third Psalm with its assurance of restoration, comfort and mercy.

> *The Lord is my shepherd; I shall not want. He maketh me to lie down in green pasture: he leadeth me beside still waters. He restoreth my soul: he leadeth me in the paths of righteousness for his name's sake. Yea, though I walk through the valley of the shadow of death, I will fear no evil: for thou art with me; thy rod and thy staff they comfort me. Thou preparest a table before me in the presence of mine enemies: thou anointest my head with oil; my cup runneth over. Surely goodness and mercy shall follow me all the days of my life: and I will dwell in the house of the LORD for ever.*

Dear God, move us through our days of grief, that the journey be one of understanding and acceptance. Let us not tarry nor detour in misery and blame, but arrive in due measure at Your house in joy. Amen.

15

Harriet Lane

"The perfect combination of deference and grace"

Meet Harriet

Born	Franklin County, Pennsylvania, 1830
Married	Henry Elliott Johnson, 1866
Children	Two sons
First Lady	1857-1861
Died	1903 at age 73
Harriet's World	South Carolina secedes from the Union; Civil War breaks out; Pony Express begins mail service to California; the game of croquet is introduced from England and becomes popular.

First Ladies have not always been the wives of the sitting presidents. When a president has been widowed or when the First Lady has been unable or unwilling to serve, then assistance from another hostess has always been employed in the social duties of the White House. Among these "substitute" hostesses, Harriet Lane holds such unique status that she is frequently included in the list of "official" First Ladies. She was the niece of the only bachelor president—James Buchanan. She served as his First Lady in every capacity throughout his entire administration. So although she was not his wife, she was most certainly his helpmate. She ran his household.

Harriet Lane had been orphaned at age 11, and was reared under the care of her legal guardian, James Buchanan. She affectionately called him, "Nunc." He called her, "Hal." His investment in her education paid off, for she grew into a poised, captivating friend and political asset in his career. By the time he was Secretary of State, she was a full partner in social gatherings. In fact, when she joined him in London, Queen Victoria appointed her to the rank of "ambassador's wife."

"Nunc" was elected president of the United States in 1857, and "Hal" took over the White House as First Lady. Washington society and the country, bored from years of dour, sorrowful Pierce administration, were enchanted by her gaiety and enthusiasm that filled the White House with flowers and filled the rooms with guests. Harriet was hailed as the "Democratic Queen,"

and even had a song written in her honor: "Listen to the Mockingbird." The timing was perfect because Buchanan stepped into the Oval Office at the same time the country was being torn apart over the issue of slavery and states' rights. Harriet became masterful at arranging seating at the dining table so that opposing factions could avoid conflict over the soup course. As good as she was at it, no amount of social acumen could forestall the war; and Buchanan's administration was marred by seven states seceding.

Harriet Lane eventually met and married Henry Elliot Johnston, a banker from Baltimore. Her uncle, who had earlier warned her against "rushing precipitately into matrimonial connexions," approved. Within 18 years, she lost "Nunc," Henry, and both of her sons.

Her legacy is two-fold. When she died, she left a large art collection to the American government, inspiring an official of the Smithsonian to declare her "First Lady of the National Collection of Fine Arts." She also bequeathed a large sum of money to Johns Hopkins Hospital in Baltimore, founding a pediatric center that is today one of the premier clinics in the country: The Harriet Lane Outpatient Clinic.

Very little is known about Harriet Lane's specific faith, but we can certainly say that she was a giving woman, who lived well in service to her family and her country, even unto death.

Lessons from Harriet

"And whosoever shall compel you to go a mile, go with him two (Matthew 5:41).

Harriet stepped into the role of First Lady to help her uncle during one of the most divisive periods in American history. With her help, the president was able to concentrate on administration while still enjoying the obvious benefits of a hospitable home to which he could bring political friends and foes to break bread together. Harriet also healed the sorrow of the previous administration by bringing in fresh enthusiasm and energy. None of this was her "duty." She was not Buchanan's wife. But she was his grateful niece and loving friend, and in that spirit, she worked tirelessly on his behalf. The lesson we learn from her is to reach out when someone needs help. Put your own needs aside for a little while, and lend a helping hand. Both you and the person you help will be richly blessed.

Dear God, help us to serve the people who share our lives. Please help us to do it in joy and with the sacrificial love of Christ for as long as You would have us there. Amen.

16

Mary Todd Lincoln

"If I erred in judgment, God forgive me."
Mary Lincoln on her deathbed

Meet Mary

Born	Kentucky, 1818
Married	Abraham Lincoln, 1842
Children	4 sons (one died at 4, one at 11, one at 18)
First Lady	1861–1865
Died	1882 at age 63
Mary's World	The Civil War divides the nation; the thirteenth Amendment abolishes slavery; the Red Cross is established; "In God We Trust" is placed on coins for the first time.

Looking back from the 21st century, we view Mary Todd Lincoln as a tragic figure besieged with multiple illnesses of which there was little understanding and for which there were no cures. Forensic historians today think she might have been diabetic and probably suffered from compulsive disorders, depression and other recurring mental illnesses. But to the public of her day, she was simply an arrogant, selfish, vain, crude, meddlesome person.

No First Lady suffered as much abuse as Mary did from every side. Her quirky demeanor won her few friends, but her idle chatter and gossip sounded the death knell on her reputation. She had a bad habit of repeating things she heard in confidence in the White House. During the Civil War, she was accused of being a spy by the North and a traitor by the South. Sensitive to the political implications of a president with a wife who couldn't be discrete, Abraham Lincoln simply stopped confiding even the smallest bits of information to her. Confused by the impact of remarks innocently made and the stonewalling from her husband, Mary grew increasingly isolated. Her one comfort was shopping. She would travel to New York, where dressmakers and milliners, flattered to be patronized by the First Lady, fluttered all over her, making her feel important and interesting. They also made her feel beautiful in

Mrs. Lincoln and her sons, Tad and Willie.

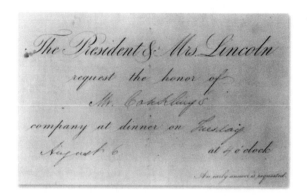

A dinner invitation issued by the Lincolns.

the finery they fashioned for her. She loved it. She indulged. She plunged the Lincolns into debt. Almost worse was the reaction of the appalled American public, which regarded such extravagant spending as heretical during wartime, when so many were starving and without homes. Mary grew even more isolated and depressed.

When the Lincolns' son Willie died, already emotionally fragile, she suffered a mental collapse. But even the image of a grief-stricken mother did nothing to bring sympathy or relief from the attacks on her character by the public. Her days of entertaining in the White House were over, which brought more criticism—this time of shirking her responsibilities. Perhaps Mary hardly noticed. She had, by then, turned inward, and was busy with spiritualists and seances to contact Willie.

Mary was born into a wealthy family of seven children. Her mother died when she was seven and her father remarried the following year. She had a good formal education and met Lincoln while staying with her sister in Springfield. She enjoyed Springfield and was a popular and pretty lass, known for her bright conversation. Her brother-in-law claimed, "Mary could make a bishop forget his prayers." Although Lincoln was "the plainest looking man in Springfield," Mary recognized his potential and bypassed other suitors to marry him in 1842.

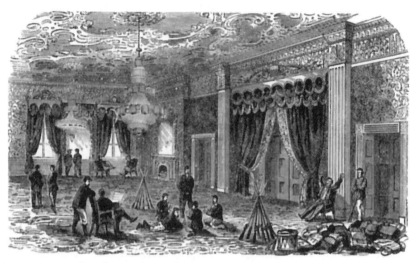

Troops quartered in the East Room during the Civil War.

Despite her fits of anger, jealousy, and depression, Lincoln remained devoted to her and largely understanding throughout their marriage. Once after an especially loud and angry outburst from her, a friend asked Lincoln why he didn't do something. He shrugged and calmly replied that her outbursts did no harm and seemed to do her some good. His dry wit and patience were the perfect complements to her erratic character. Commenting on her wealthy background, Lincoln said. "One 'd' is good enough for God, but not for the Todds."

Mary was able to provide help during the war by visiting wounded solders, some of whom actually camped in the East Room of the White House. She had a morbid fear that her oldest son or husband would be killed.

Things were looking brighter in 1865 with Lincoln's reelection, General Lee's surrender and the collapse of the Confederacy—at least bright enough to venture forth for a night at the theater. Mary's premonitions and fears were all realized right before her eyes as she saw her husband shot. Mary was grief-stricken for months and became even more unstable and paranoid and tortured by a suspicion that she was destitute (untrue). She fled to Europe for six years with her son Tad, but he died in 1871 at only 18. One son, Robert, remained. He was forced to hospitalize his mother for mental illness in 1875. Mary lived for 17 years after the assassination, but never fully recovered. As the minister proclaimed at her funeral, the "bullet that sped its way and took her husband from earth, took her also."

Mary grew up in a religious family. The Todds attended the Presbyterian Church every Sunday. When Mary moved to Springfield, she attended the Episcopal Church. Although Mary claimed to believe in predestination, she always tried to change her destiny and persuade God to see things her way. Abraham Lincoln never joined a church and seldom attended services, but he daily sought refuge in the Bible and was a very spiritual person. Mary also read her Bible, but it didn't bring her comfort or guidance. One story describes how Mary had walked to church, mostly to see her friends and show off her dress, while Lincoln stayed outside, pulling their youngsters around in a little wagon and reading his Bible. When Mary came out from church, she found one of the children crying beside the sidewalk and Abe calmly pulling the wagon far down the street. He was so engrossed in his reading that he didn't realize he had lost one of his flock. Mary had been in church, but Abe had been in the spirit.

Lessons from Mary

And the cares of this world, and the deceitfulness of riches, and the lusts of other things entering in, choke the word, and it becometh unfruitful (Mark 4:19).

Every kingdom divided against itself is brought to desolation, and every city or house divided against itself shall not stand (Matthew 12:25).

Those that hate me without cause are more than the hairs of my head (Psalm 69:4).

It was probably easy to despise and ridicule Mary. She was a jealous, self-centered whiner. It was also probably possible to admire Mary. She was a charming, gracious hostess, and quick-witted and loyal companion to a husband who suffered severe bouts of depression. The real Mary was both, but she was also a woman whose illnesses were undiagnosed and incurable in the 1800s. Today we can recognize and treat mental illness, but the sufferers are still ridiculed, shunned, and misunderstood. We need to accept and care for the mentally ill, just as we care for any other person of need. They are no less worthy, but most needy of our concern and understanding.

Dear God, we come to You as "the least of these" and beg Your forgiveness. Grant us acceptance, understanding, and willingness to work with and for all people. Amen.

17

Eliza McCardle Johnson

"A loyal White House recluse"

▩ Meet Eliza

Born	Tennessee, 1810
Married	Andrew Johnson, 1827
Children	Five
First Lady	1865-1869
Died	1876 at age 65
Eliza's World	First transcontinental railroad is completed; Congress authorizes a five-cent coin called a "nickel;" first fire department with paid firefighters is established in New York City; Edison patents an electric voting machine.

Young Eliza must have had a good eye for good men. The day she first saw Andrew Johnson (future president of the United States), she announced to her girlfriend that she just might marry "that boy." "That boy" was a ragged, unemployed teenager who was leading a blind donkey pulling a cart through the dirt streets of Greeneville, Tennessee, looking for work as a tailor. She married him within the year.

When they met, Andrew could barely read or write. Eliza taught him the basics, and he hired a man to read to him as he worked in his tailor shop. Hard work paid off. Her husband, Andrew Johnson, served in the Tennessee legislature, the US Congress, as governor of Tennessee and as vice president under Abraham Lincoln. He had had a good career.

Eliza had never liked politics and had remained at home for more than 20 years of Johnson's career. He was known as a very moral man who supported the Union, even though he was from Tennessee. This had won him the admiration (and the vice presidency) of Abraham Lincoln, but also garnered the hatred and wrath of his fellow Southern countrymen. When word came that President Lincoln had been assassinated, Eliza feared for her husband's safety as he stepped into the presidency, and finally moved to Washington and into the White House with her extended family. She was 55 years old and suffering from tuberculosis. Because of Eliza's illness, her daughter assumed duties as White House hostess and did a remarkable job, despite the looting and shambles of the White House after the assassination. Eliza only made two public appearances in her four years in the White House, one of those for her husband's sixtieth birthday party.

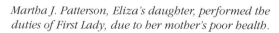

Martha J. Patterson, Eliza's daughter, performed the duties of First Lady, due to her mother's poor health.

Unfortunately, Abraham Lincoln was a hard act to follow. President Johnson was a very unpopular president and when he broke one of the imposed rules of the Republican's Reconstruction Plan after the Civil War, he was the first president to be impeached. He was acquitted by one vote, but his career was ruined.

The Johnsons left Washington in 1869 and returned to Tennessee, but retirement was no less tragic. Their son died six weeks after they returned home, and Andrew ran for Congress and was defeated twice. Andrew and Eliza died within six months of each other in 1875 and 1876. They had enjoyed a good marriage for almost 50 years.

As is true with many of the early First Ladies, very little is known about Eliza as a person. Her father died when she was young and her mother supported the family by making and selling quilts. One could assume that she had little education.

After she married, she proved to be a very efficient manager of the family businesses and farm. With Andrew away for long periods of time in elected offices, she raised and educated the children alone. The two daughters were healthy and well adjusted, but the youngest son also suffered from tuberculosis and the two oldest boys became alcoholics. As her husband did, she remained loyal to the Union throughout the Civil War, even when her home was taken by the Confederates and her life was in danger.

She was a Methodist and a supporter of the poor and working class. She attended church, and it is assumed that she attended with her husband. He preferred to attend a different church every Sunday. He especially liked the Catholic Church because the children were dressed in uniforms and people could not distinguish the poor child from the rich one. Even in the White House the Johnsons never forgot their humble beginnings and how hard it was to be poor and struggling.

Lessons from Eliza

Who can find a virtuous woman? For her price is far above rubies. The heart of her husband doth safely trust in her, so that he shall have no need of spoil (Proverbs 31:10-11).

Eliza tried hard to avoid the political world. She stayed home, reared her children, and managed the family businesses while Johnson served in elected offices in his town, the state capital, and finally in Washington. Even when Johnson served as vice president under Lincoln, Eliza had no plans to move to Washington and become a political partner. But Eliza was a devoted wife and knowing that Andrew was already unpopular and that a deranged man had shot the popular president, she understandably feared for her husband's safety. When Lincoln was assassinated, Eliza quickly packed up and moved to Washington. She put her own health aside to be with her husband. From Eliza we learn devotion and dedication. She met her love when he was a ragged, semi-literate, unemployed boy, and never gave up on him. From tailor to president! Only in America and only with the help of a dedicated wife.

Dear God, **help us to see a president in every ragged child. For by seeing a bright and shining future in every person, we will provide the care and love, and with your support, it will happen. Amen.**

18

Julia Dent Grant

"She shared his trials and his triumphs, his sorrows and his joys."

Meet Julia

Born	Missouri, 1826
Married	Ulysses S. Grant, 1848
Children	Four (three sons, one daughter)
First Lady	1869-1877
Died	1902 at age 76
Julia's World	Jehovah's Witnesses are established; Yellowstone National Park opens; cable cars are invented for San Francisco; the first Chautauqua Assembly meets at Chautauqua Lake, New York to train church workers and Sunday school teachers.

Among the early First Ladies, Julia Grant is distinguished as having written a memoir late in her life (although it was not published until 1975). Because she tells much of her own story, we have to rely only a little on historians for insight into her inner life.

For Julia Grant, life was a long series of ups and downs as she followed her famous husband through failure and fanfare. Ulysses S. Grant was known as a butcher, a drunkard and the most celebrated hero of the Civil War. Through it all, Julia stood by her "Ulys"—cheerful and supportive, almost oblivious to disasters falling around her.

Julia was born into a wealthy family on a large farm near St. Louis, Missouri. She had a formal education at a boarding school for affluent girls for seven years. She describes her youth as "one long summer of sunshine, flowers, and smiles ..." In 1843, she met Grant when he visited her home as a guest of her brother, both on break from West Point. For Grant it was love at first sight. And Julia couldn't get him out of her thoughts. But the families had second thoughts. Her father did not approve of Grant because a regular Army officer would never be able to support his daughter in the manner to which she was accustomed. Grant's family did not

Because of the entertaining in which Julia Grant engaged, she maintained several different sets of china. Pictured here are pieces from the private set she used for her family.

approve of Julia, because the Dent family owned slaves. Somehow Ulys and Julia overcame familial objections (at least, Julia's family's), and Julia accepted his engagement ring. The Mexican War delayed their wedding for four years, but they were married finally in 1848. Grant's parents did not attend the ceremony.

The Grants entertained lavishly in the Gilded Age.

The early years were hard for young wife Julia, not only due to poverty, constant travel, and bleak military quarters in distant garrisons, but also because of Grant's excessive drinking. Julia managed to get him to join a temperance lodge, but his drinking periods intensified when he was transferred to the West Coast and Julia returned to her parents' home to await his return.

Grant resigned from the military and tried farming, logging, tanning, and real estate, but all his business ventures were failures. Julia held the family together and managed to deliver and rear four healthy children. The outbreak of the Civil War actually saved Grant. He returned to the Army and quickly rose in rank and reputation. Julia and the children went with him on most of his assignments, and Julia even permitted the oldest son, then 13, to ride into battle with his father.

Grant, the war hero, easily won the presidency of the United States. He was the youngest president to date. But while his administration was successful on several fronts, in other ways it struggled with scandal. His cabinet was rife with graft and corruption, and many of his appointees took personal advantage of the naiveté of the Grants. In spite of the embarrassing and damaging difficulties of the Grant administration, Julia was light and joyful. After years of slogging around military garrisons, she loved the White House and Washington society loved her. She entertained lavishly and often, hosting five state receptions and the White House wedding of their daughter, Nellie.

After leaving the White House, the Grants moved to New York. When a partner defrauded an investment firm co-owned by their son, the Grants were faced with poverty and debt beyond their means to pay. Ulysses began writing his memoirs to raise enough money to keep his family afloat financially. Time was of the essence, because he had throat cancer and knew he was dying. He completed the work, but died before it was published. Family friend, Mark Twain, took over and published the book, yielding $450,000 for Julia and their family. Ironically and nearly poetically, Grant's financial success came after he died and in his final, sacrificial, loving work on this earth.

Surrounded by her children and grandchildren, Julia lived seventeen years after her beloved Ulys died. She also developed a close friendship with Varina Davis, the widow of Jefferson Davis, President of the Confederacy. How ironic, yet fitting, that the widows of the two prominent opposing figures in the Civil War should find friendship. Many families and friends separated by the war were never able to reconcile even decades after the war. Julia Grant and Varina Davis knew the meaning of the word, "forgiveness."

Julia was a Methodist and regularly attended church. When the Grants left the White House in 1877, they embarked on a two-year around-the-world odyssey. She fulfilled her life-long dream of visiting the Holy Lands. In her memoir, she stated that she felt the presence of God in the Garden of Gesthemane and that she prayed and pleaded for mercy in Bethany and Jerusalem. She lived her faith also by never giving up on Grant, even in his lapses and his failures. She was always there and always understanding. In a letter to her son, she summed up her philosophy: "The only way to get along is to take the world as you find it and make the best of it."

Lessons from Julia

Blessed are the merciful; for they shall obtain mercy (Matthew 5:7).

But I say unto you, Love your enemies, bless them that curse you, do good to them that hate you, and pray for them which despitefully use you, and persecute you (Matthew 5:44).

Pleasant words are as a honeycomb, sweet to the soul, and health to the bones (Proverbs 16:24).

For Julia the glass was always half full ... no, perhaps overflowing. She loved her life wherever she happened to land. It wasn't all roses, but somehow she always made a bouquet. From Julia we learn the simple, but profound lesson of attitude. We can shape our lives much more than they can shape us. We grow and become stronger from days in the hot seat, not days in the hammock. A modern day example is a veteran school principal who was excited over appointment to an old inner city school. A friend asked her how she could possibly be happy about a move to a school that was falling down, had no supplies, a high failure rate, and terrible morale and turnover. "Yes," the principal replied, "Isn't it wonderful? Look at all the progress we can make!" Julia saw Ulysses as such a challenge, met with love and a great sense of adventure. Look at all the progress he made.

Dear God, help us to bloom where we are planted. There are gifts and great lessons to be found in all things, and we can be your nurturers and messengers if You will just strengthen us. Use us, Lord. Amen.

19

Lucy Ware Webb Hayes

The White House is "whiter and purer because Mrs. Hayes has been its mistress." **Unitarian Minister**

Meet Lucy

Born	Ohio, 1831
Married	Rutherford B. Hayes, 1852
Children	Eight (three died in infancy)
First Lady	1877-1881
Died	1889 at age 57
Lucy's World	Reconstruction ends in the South; Woolworth's opens its first store; the artificial sweetener Saccharin is discovered.

Lucy became the First Lady under very uncertain circumstances. When the election of Rutherford B. Hayes as President of the United States should have been whipping Washington into an Inaugural frenzy of celebration and oath-taking, all was subdued. In point of fact, the outcome of the election was in serious question. Hayes had been elected in a hotly contested battle wherein the Democrats won the majority vote, but the Republicans were accused of buying electoral votes in the South. The Electoral Commission was deadlocked until March and then voted along strict party lines, giving the election to Hayes by one vote. President Hayes was defiled, ridiculed and labeled "Rutherfraud." While the results of the election were being verified, the Inaugural Ball had to be cancelled. So Lucy's entry into the White House was tinted with public doubt and outrage ... and a large measure of personal dignity and serenity on Lucy's part.

Lucy Hayes photographed with new photography technique — halo oval framing.

Lucy was the daughter of a doctor who died while on a trip to free slaves belonging to his family. Lucy and her brothers were educated in private schools and Lucy was the first woman to attend Ohio Wesleyan College (graduating from Wesleyan Female College in Cincinnati at age 18), and the first First Lady to receive a college degree.

Lucy's mother actually worked to arrange an introduction with 'Ruddy' Hayes, a lawyer and the son of a church friend. He was encouraged to pay calls at the Webb home to spend time with Lucy. In spite of this matchmaking, Lucy and Rutherford fell in love. He would write in his diary, "By George! I am in love with her."

"Here, we are all on one level."
Lucy Hayes,
while in church

They married after she completed college. Lucy traveled with Rutherford during the Civil War, during which time he grew to share her religious conviction that slavery was wrong. When he was in command of the 23rd Ohio Volunteer Infantry, she ministered to the wounded, comforted the dying, and visited the homesick. They nicknamed her "Mother Lucy." Some of the wounded soldiers remembered her fourteen years later by sending her a memorial gift to the White House for the Rutherfords' 25th wedding anniversary celebration.

When war hero Rutherford Hayes was elected to Congress and three terms as Ohio's governor, Lucy accompanied him to prisons, reform schools and asylums. Her position as wife to a congressman and later a governor gave her wide access for spreading her faith. It also gave her experience that would later serve her well as First Lady of the United States.

Although First Lady Lucy Hayes strongly opposed slavery and alcohol and believed in the rights of women, she never joined any action groups or made any public statements supporting social causes. In spite of her silence, Lucy was politically astute. She did not speak publicly for the suffrage or temperance movements because she knew her endorsement would be detrimental to her husband's career. Allegiance to her husband came first. She simply "walked the talk," and became a much admired and respected First Lady.

However, she did make her positions known ... quietly. Because of their lifelong Christian beliefs, the Hayes family did not serve any alcohol in the White House. Hayes made the decision, but Lucy won the nickname, "Lemonade Lucy." They also wanted to send a message to the country that alcohol was destroying people and families, and if the White House could exist without alcohol, so could any home. Even though Lucy did not formally join their organization, her actions spoke legions and the Women's Christian Temperance Union commissioned a life-size portrait to be painted in her honor. The charming portrait included a small female figure in bas-relief in the background pouring water from a vase. A subtle message, but loud and clear.

Lemonade Lucy managed to combine piety and popularity. She instituted daily morning worship services, Bible readings, and Sunday night hymn singing. The Hayes family was Methodist and walked to church together every Sunday. Lucy saved the custom of the Children's Easter Egg Roll by inviting the children to the White House Lawn. (Previously, it been held on the Capitol lawn, but cranky Congressmen complained that it ruined the lawn.) The Hayes also celebrated their 25th wedding anniversary by renewing

White gown worn by Lucy Hayes.

their vows in a White House ceremony. Lucy wore her original wedding gown (certainly an impressive feat after eight pregnancies) and they had their original attendants (no record if the bridesmaids could also fit into their original gowns). They concluded their anniversary with a huge public reception. Lucy truly loved the White House and cried so hard when she left that her husband remarked he was surprised she "didn't leave claw marks."

Working in hospitals and for the poor, helping to establish an orphans' home, and living simply and frugally throughout her life, Lucy was a true servant of God. Hayes declined a second term, and the family retired to Ohio. Lucy continued her good works by teaching Sunday School, hosting church suppers and serving as president of the Methodist Woman's Home Missionary Society. She died of a stroke in 1889, surrounded by her family. Hayes wrote in his diary, "She is in heaven. She is where all the best of earth have gone."

Lessons from Lucy

But we will give ourselves continually to prayer, and to the ministry of the word (Acts 6:4).

He that hath two coats, let him impart to him that hath none (Luke 3:11).

Lucy put her faith into action. She was not afraid to demonstrate her religion and to live by it, even in the White House. Despite political scandals, Lucy was never personally attacked. She stood on higher ground. And although doubt and public dissention swirled around the Hayes presidential administration, Lucy exuded the integrity, piety, purity, sincerity, and genuine love to which every Christian would aspire. It wouldn't be hard to imagine that her daily prayer might have been as Jesus prayed, "Forgive them, Lord. For they know not what they do." And she put her faith into action. In spite of the anger of their enemies, she stayed in service to God with time, talents, goods, and example.

Dear God, please direct our feet on the higher road. Help us to light candles to show the way out of darkness. Make us generous in our gifts and our time. Amen.

20

Lucretia Rudolph Garfield

"I need not be the shrinking slave of toil,
but could be its regal master." Crete Garfield

Meet Crete

Born	Ohio, 1832
Married	James A. Garfield, 1858
Children	Seven (two died in childhood)
First Lady	1881
Died	1918 at the age of 85
Lucretia's World	Salvation Army is established in Philadelphia; Booker T. Washington becomes president of the college later known as Tuskegee Institute; Barnum and Bailey create their circus; the Boston Symphony Orchestra is founded.

It was not love at first sight for Lucretia ("Crete") Rudolf and James Garfield. It was more a matter of an enamored student and a teacher's pet. They first met in a seminary in 1849 and again in 1851 at the Western Reserve Eclectic Institute, where James was Crete's Latin teacher. Under the tutelage of handsome James, Crete took a more than serious interest in Latin and learned it so well that she was able to teach her children years later. And the young Latin professor had not only a devoted student, but also a girlfriend.

However, James wasn't sure that his pretty, shy Latin student had the gaiety and passion for which he was looking in a mate. He needed time to think. James went off to teach in Massachusetts while Crete remained in Cleveland, where she, too, took a teaching position. They courted long distance. After an "understanding" of nine years, they finally married in 1858. After nine years, one would assume that the Garfields were secure in their relationship, but evidently the absence that had made their hearts grow fonder didn't help their early years as man and wife. After their first four years together, James declared that the marriage was a mistake, perhaps, in part, because life in general was proving challenging for him. By this time he had served in the Civil War, contracted malaria, returned to Ohio and entered politics.

In 1867 the Garfields moved to Washington where James served in Congress for seventeen years. Theirs were the quiet lives of academics. They both belonged to the Washington Literary Society, but were active in little else.

Crete was surprised and frightened at the nomination of her husband to the presidency, but she was poised and supportive throughout the campaign and election. They moved into the White House in March, 1881, but had little time to settle in. Crete contracted malaria and went to the New Jersey shore to recuperate.

While on his way to visit his ailing wife in July, Garfield was shot by an assassin. Crete was continually by his side during the two months he lingered near death in the White House. She convinced the physician and assistants to bring in troughs of ice and fans to create the first "air conditioning machine" in an attempt to lower the high summer temperatures in the White House and make James more comfortable. They did manage to lower the temperature a few degrees, but Garfield died of his wounds and blood poisoning at the end of the summer. He was only 49 years old. Crete lived another 36 years.

Crete was an intelligent, independent woman who didn't have enough time to have much historical significance in the White House. The few months she had were marred by her illness and James' assassination. What little we do know of her is that she was well educated and insisted that her children were, as well. They had seven children, but two died at very early ages. The other five lived long and successful lives.

We know that the Garfields' marriage was difficult. Although Crete clearly loved James, she was apparently not outwardly emotional or expressive. Her husband sought company with other women, and, as many wives might, she blamed herself. The death of their young daughter did draw them closer to each other, and by the time they entered the White House, they realized and appreciated their uniqueness and their love. Crete had acquiesced to the role of political wife and devoted mother, and James had finally seen the warmth and concern that she had kept hidden, at no time more evident than the last two months of his life as she fought to save him.

Crete was reared in a strongly religious family, and she and James were members of the Disciples of Christ when they were married. James actually served as a minister for a short period of time. Her conviction to God gave her a clear sense of justice. She had the courage to strongly oppose slavery. She also indicated early concerns for women's rights, but did not support the suffrage movement, which would later lead to legislation that would give women the right to vote. That she didn't support it is not surprising. She lived in a time when husbands spoke for their wives. In fact, even if a woman worked outside her home, her paycheck was made payable to her husband or her father. It was unthinkable that a wife might oppose her husband's stance on any matter, including political candidates. So giving women the right to vote would, at the very least, be redundant; the wife would vote the same as her husband, giving each man two identical votes in an election. Both she and James thought so. At the very worst, they thought that allowing women the independence to vote would destroy the delicate balance of power within the home and family. Crete, earlier a teacher with an impressive education, gave up her own career to care for and defend her family as a wife and mother.

Lessons from Crete

So ought men to love their wives as their own bodies. He that loveth his wife loveth himself (Ephesians 6:28).

Is any sick among you? Let him call for the elders of the church, and let them pray over him, anointing him with oil in the name of the Lord (James 5:14).

Crete reminds us that no one ever said love was easy. Most relationships go through periods of doubt, sometimes even distrust and betrayal, but love keeps us together. And the adversities can also be the adhesives.

Severe loss and adversity change marriages simply because the people are changed. Some people fall apart, destroying their relationships in the process. How often have we read or heard of divorces that followed the death of a child or some catastrophic event? But it doesn't have to be that way. The better way to handle grief is to draw closer to God and to the people who love you, so that they can support you in your vulnerability. James and Crete moved closer together. Only then did he see her soft side. He realized that she did love him despite her inability to openly display warmth and affection, but it took the death of their child before James really understood how deeply she cared and how completely she loved.

Dear God, **teach us to be open to each other and love each other with the tender, protective love of Christ. Give us the strength to be weak so that You and the people who share our lives can help us. When we see pain, give us the courage to move in without regard for our own comfort or convenience. Amen.**

21

Ellen Lewis Herndon Arthur

"Her voice and manner won the praises of those who heard her."

◈ *Meet Ellen*

Born	Virginia, 1837
Married	Chester A. Arthur, 1859
Children	Three (one died in infancy)
First Lady	Died before Arthur's election
Died	1880 at the age of 42
Ellen's World	Civil Service Reform enacted; the game of Bingo is introduced.

Ellen Arthur was a beautiful soprano soloist and the wife of an affluent politician. She had accepted an invitation to a benefit concert in New York City on a cold January night in 1880. Her husband, Chester, declined to accompany her, choosing instead to handle political matters in Albany. While waiting for a carriage, alone in the sleet, Ellen Arthur caught a chill, developed pneumonia, and died in a matter of days. She was only 42. Guilt-ridden that he had not been there to offer his coat or hail the carriage faster or protect her from the weather, Chester spiraled into inexpressible grief. He kept her room as she had left it and placed flowers in front of a hand-tinted, silver-framed photograph every day of his life. Even the triumph of being nominated as vice president of the United States on a winning ticket and elected the following November did nothing to soften his grief.

Like Presidents Tyler, Fillmore and Johnson before him, Chester Arthur suddenly became president after the death of the elected president, James Garfield. Unlike his three predecessors, Arthur was a widower, so he had no First Lady. He would give no woman that honor that should have been his wife's. While he was in office, his sister, Mary Arthur McElroy, served as the official hostess of the White House for certain events and helped care for his daughter. Although not a bad president, he was portrayed as a dandy, more

concerned with his expensive suits and wines than with the needs of the country. He was not reelected. He never remarried and lived less than seven years after Ellen's death, dying at 56.

Mary McElroy, President Arthur's sister, served as official White House hostess during his administration.

Death by Fashion

Ellen's was a death that can be directly attributed to fashion. Ladies of the era prized a flattened bodice, a tiny waist, and a derriere accentuated by a bustle. To achieve this hourglass shape, women resorted to mechanical means: laced corsets reinforced with metal or bone rods, called stays. Both the corsets and the bodices of the dresses had stays. Women typically had assistance dressing, and the corsets were pulled tight by the laces until the woman gasped for breath. Inability to breathe was considered a fair price to pay for fashion. When the female body is cinched at the waist, the lungs and stomach are pressed up, the diaphragm is pressed in, and the intestines and uterus are pressed down. Not being able to draw a deep breath, meant that a woman couldn't cough or clear her lungs. It didn't take long in this condition for a slight cold to become pneumonia. Fainting and the "vapors" were the signatures of refined ladies of the day, but in reality they were critical medical conditions caused by the lack of oxygen. Stay were even worn throughout pregnancy and only expanded slightly to accommodate a growing baby. The constricted uterus had to contribute to difficulties in pregnancies. Although there are no medical statistics, it is generally believed that stays caused miscarriages, still births, and infant mortality.

These fashion statements also directly impaired women's muscle tone and movement. Women, held up and in by stays, eventually lost their own ability to sit and stand without assistance. Fashion also dictated that a woman in the public eye change her clothes four to six times a day. Thus, cinching was not only tortuous, it was unceasing. Although this fashion was debilitating and sometimes deadly, most First Ladies prevailed and were accomplished partners in their husband's administrations in spite of this small problem of breathing. As one First Lady wryly noted, "It's hard to be a trail-blazer if you don't know where your next breath is coming from."

Ellen was a beautiful, talented woman who met young Arthur in New York City. She was the daughter of a fallen Navy hero and enjoyed the city social scene. Arthur was a promising lawyer. They wed in 1859. Ellen was obviously a very accomplished soprano, listed as a soloist on several programs. She joined the Mendelssohn Glee Club, and their rehearsals and concerts occupied much of her time. She also had three children in ten years. Unfortunately, the youngest died when he was only two years old. In 1878, her mother died and Ellen became depressed and never recovered.

What little is known of Ellen reveals an entertaining, socially astute woman, who would have excelled as a First Lady in the White House. She loved to entertain and supported charitable concerts and programs.

She was an Episcopalian, but virtually nothing else is known of her faith. After Arthur became president, he dedicated a stained glass window in her memory at St. John's Episcopal Church, a window he could view from the White House.

Lesson from Ellen

Let the word of Christ dwell in you richly in all wisdom; teaching and admonishing one another in Psalms and hymns and spiritual songs, singing with grace in your hearts to the Lord (Colossians 3:14).

I returned and saw under the sun, that the race is not to the swift, nor the battle to the strong, neither yet bread to the wise, nor yet riches to men of understanding, nor yet favor to men of skill; but time and chance happen to them all (Ecclesiastes 9:11).

From Ellen we see again the tragedy of a young life taken before she ever had a chance to really use her time or talents. Ellen had a beautiful voice and shared it not only in a professional manner, but also for benefits and charity concerts. But, like all of us, she had no idea her time was so short. People who recover from serious illness are frequently thankful for the illness, because it helps them appreciate the life they have been given. We *can* learn to savor and appreciate each and every day as a special gift from God without a near-death experience, but it takes a little time and a little prayer.

Dear God, we know not how many of these beautiful 24-hour gifts we will receive from You, but guide us in opening, using, and closing each one with a small prayer of thanks. Amen.

22 and 24

❧❀❧

Frances Folsom Cleveland

"She carries sunshine wherever she goes."

▩ *Meet Frances*

Born	New York, 1864
Married	Grover Cleveland, 1886
Children	Five (one died in childhood)
First Lady	1886-1889 and 1893-1897
Died	1947 at age 83
Frances' World	The Statue of Liberty, a gift from France, is dedicated in New York harbor; yellow fever epidemic kills 400 in Florida; Sears and Roebuck starts its mail-order catalogue business; first Sunday comics appear.

The Cleveland's tale reads like a story out of the tabloids instead of the history books. Grover Cleveland was a confirmed bachelor and a lawyer in Buffalo when his law partner died in an accident. Cleveland was the administrator of his partner's estate and acted as guardian for his partner's 11-year-old daughter, Frances Folsom. (When was a baby, he bought little "Frank's" first baby carriage.) Cleveland entered politics and served as mayor of Buffalo and governor of New York before being nominated for president in 1884. Cleveland won the nomination and entered the presidency as a bachelor. Although he was not physically fit or handsome, he was the most eligible bachelor in the country, and rumors and matchmaking flourished.

Rose Elizabeth Cleveland served as White House hostess for her bachelor brother during 15 months of his first term in office.

When 21 year-old "Frank" and her mother visited the White House in 1885, most assumed the mother was a prospect, but the rumors ended in 1886 when Grover Cleveland, age 49, married his former ward Frances, age 21 in a magnificent ceremony in the White House. Frances Folsom Cleveland was the first bride of a President to be married in the White House. She was also the youngest First Lady. Despite differences in their ages and personalities, the marriage was a success and they had five children in the 22 years they were wed.

The public loved Frances Cleveland. She was a real-life Cinderella—young and beautiful, and the perfect hostess. While Frances loved the White House and reveled in the public attention, the same did not hold true for her husband. The press was unkind. In his bid for reelection, he was accused of being a wife-beater, and Frances had to publicly refute the outrageous charges. Cleveland lost his reelection to Benjamin Harrison, but Frances wasn't tired of

On June 2, 1886, President Grover Cleveland married Miss Frances Folsom in the Blue Room of the White House. Frances was the daughter of his former law partner.

the White House yet. She told the White House staff to take good care of everything while she was gone, because she and Grover would be back in four years. She was good to her word, and Cleveland became the first and only president to win a second, non-consecutive presidential term. Their first child "Baby Ruth" became a celebrity when they reentered the White House and her

sister Ester became the first baby to actually be born in the White House. Frances had another daughter and two sons, the last one born when she was 39 and Cleveland 66.

"Frank" became so popular that woman's clubs sprang up in her honor and the media spied on her and the children day and night. One visitor on the White House lawn tried to cut a lock of baby Ester's hair for a souvenir. In frustration, Cleveland bought a house in Washington and the family actually lived in their private home, "Red Top," most of the time, only appearing at the White House for work and social functions. After leaving the White House, they retired to Princeton, where Cleveland died at age 71. Frances survived him by almost 40 years. In 1913, she remarried and stayed active until she died suddenly at age 83.

Frances was a Presbyterian and believed in temperance and charity. In a biography written in 1889, she was described as a religious and gracious woman who "reproached wine-bibbers only by her abstinence." She was the president of the Needlework Guild of America for many years and worked to distribute nearly two million garments to needy people during the Depression. She held receptions on Saturdays so working women could attend and decreed that no one worked on Sunday. She worked for educational opportunities for girls, music scholarships, and food drives for poor local children. Frances was not only faithful, but put her faith into action making her world a better place.

Lessons from Frances

And above all things put on charity, which is the bond of perfectness (Colossians 3:14).

Every man according as he purposeth in his heart, so let him give; not grudgingly, or of necessity: for God loveth a cheerful giver. And God is able to make all grace abound toward you; that ye, always having all sufficiency in all things, may abound to every good work (2 Corinthians 9:7-8)

From Frances we learn the lesson of grace and purpose. Perhaps it was the early death of her father that caused Frances to grow up quickly and with maturity beyond her young years, but whatever the reason, she succeeded in the spotlight where many of her predecessors failed. Frances was adored, much as Jackie Kennedy over 60 years later. She seemed to have it all: beauty, charm, grace, and a sense of humor to hold it all together. But with all the adulation from the public and the press, Frances never lost sight of her real purposes. She stayed grounded in her faith and duty as a wife and mother. She was protective of her children, even to the point of moving out of the White House to secure their privacy. And she stood by her husband through the mud slinging and the political failures. She kept the Sabbath. Cleveland saw something in that young 21-year-old, and it was more than a pretty face. It was a beautiful soul.

Dear God, help us keep our priorities. We know we never outgrow the need for structure and guidance, no matter how high or how low we move. Keep our feet on the ground, that our minds might find purpose and our hearts discover heaven. Amen.

23

Caroline Lavinia Scott Harrison

"A tapestry of goodness, charity, and devotion"

Meet Carrie

Born	Ohio, 1832
Married	Benjamin Harrison, 1853
Children	Two (one son, one daughter)
First Lady	1889-1892
Died	1892 at age 60
Carrie's World	First *Wall Street Journal* published; zippers and drinking straws appear; George Ferris designs the Ferris Wheel; electric sewing machines and electric elevators are introduced.

A creative artist and the best housekeeper—not a combination found in ordinary women, but then Carrie Harrison was not an ordinary woman. Her father was a minister and educator and made sure that his children were well schooled. In fact, Reverend John Scott founded the Oxford Female Institute. Carrie met Ben when he was only 14 years old and a student in her father's class at Farmer's College. Theirs was a children's "puppy love" that would endure a lifetime. They corresponded and dated for the next six years until Ben completed his studies at Miami University in Oxford, Ohio (where Carrie's family just happened to have moved). They married in 1853 when she was just 21 and he 20. They moved to Indianapolis and had two children.

Ben worked long and hard to establish his law practice, but money was scarce and Carrie felt neglected. It became worse during the Civil War when Ben enlisted and was gone for three years. While he was gone, Carrie reared their children alone and threw herself into service with the Presbyterian church and a home for orphans. She developed her social skills by entertaining friends at home. And she played piano and painted. These were years of growth and independence. They were also valuable years for her husband. The war allowed Ben, the grandson of William Henry Harrison, to make a name for himself and to gain attention in the political ranks. Connections proved invaluable when combined with hard work and ambition. Ben moved from poor lawyer to Civil War general, to United States senator, to president of the United States in the next two decades.

When the Harrisons moved into the White House in 1889, they brought their children, grandchildren, a father, and a niece. Unfortunately, at the time, the White House had only five bedrooms and one bathroom. Carrie immediately drew up plans for a major expansion and renovation, but the plans were rejected by Congress. She did receive $35,000 for renovations and made major improvements including more bathrooms and extermination of the rats in the attic. Carrie was noted for having the cleanest White

In this photo, Carrie is holding a fan that she painted (shown below).

House. The Harrisons were also the first family to have electric lights, but they were afraid to touch the switches and had to find a servant to turn them off or on. Carrie introduced the first official Christmas tree in the White House and started the White House china collection. The Washington ladies loved her and she invited them into the White House for French lessons and china painting. She had her own kiln and made hundreds of tiles, candlesticks, pitchers, and cups for gifts and church bazaars. Carrie was also active in charities.

One of the most famous stories about her is that she was approached to lend her name and her influence to a fundraiser for Johns Hopkins University medical school. Carrie did a little background work before she agreed, and discovered that Johns Hopkins did not admit women. She told them that if they would admit women, she would raise money for them. Otherwise, no deal. They revamped their policies, admitted women, and Carrie went out and raised $500,000 for them.

While preparing for reelection in 1892, Carrie became seriously ill and Ben stopped his campaigning. Out of respect for Harrison and his ill wife, his opponent Cleveland also stopped campaigning. Carrie died of tuberculosis in

October, 1892 at the age of 60. Her daughter served as hostess for the remaining few months in the White House. Benjamin Harrison did not win reelection and survived her by eight years.

Carrie did not forsake her creative side for her spiritual side. She excelled in needlework and tapestries, creating notable pieces for her church, First Presbyterian, and for charity sales and shows. She worked with the Missionary Society and taught painting, music, and needlework. Although the Presbyterians did not approve of dancing, Carrie loved to dance and shamelessly put her daughter into dancing lessons. Throughout her life she shared her talents, stayed close to her church, and raised a devoted and loving family. The Indiana poet, James Whitcomb Riley wrote these simple but befitting lines upon her death:

Yet with the faith she knew
We see her still
Even as here she stood-
All that was pure and good
And sweet in womanhood-
God's will her will.

Lessons from Carrie

She looketh well to the ways of her household, and eateth not the bread of idleness (Proverbs 31:27).

But now, O Lord, thou art our father; we are the clay, and thou are our potter; and we all are the work of thy hand (Isaiah 65:8).

We are the work of God's hand and we in turn praise Him by the work of our hands. Carrie had special talents in her hands. She could make works of art that people and churches admired. Not all of the works of our hands generate such attention, but that doesn't mean they are any less worthy or deserving. The works of our hands include wiping a child's face, cooking a meal, typing a report, mowing our neighbor's yard. If we let God use our hands, all our works will be works of God. (And if you happen to burn the toast, don't worry; it's God's way of feeding the birds.)

Dear God, please use me, mold me, guide my hands to create reflections of Your kingdom in everything I touch. Amen.

25

Ida Saxton McKinley

"Nearer, my God, to Thee" Ida's favorite hymn

▦ *Meet Ida*

Born	Ohio, 1847
Married	William McKinley, 1871
Children	Two (both died in infancy)
First Lady	1897-1901
Died	1907 at age 59
Ida's World	Hawaii is made a territory of the United States; work begins on the New York Subway; International Ladies' Garment Workers Union is founded with the goal of shortening the 70-hour workweek; the life expectancy for males is 48 years and 51 years for females.

William McKinley may be remembered for the Spanish-American War, but his most remarkable accomplishments were his total dedication and concern for his wife, who, by the time they moved into the White House, was described as "the petulant invalid." He was her constant companion, and waited on her and responded to all of her needs and demands for more than thirty years. Quite simply, William McKinley loved Ida McKinley.

Ida was born in Canton, Ohio into a wealthy banking family. She received a good education and went to finishing school in Pennsylvania. Ida and Major William McKinley probably met at a church picnic in 1867, but Ida did not notice the short Major. After a tour of Europe, Ida returned to Canton and worked in her father's bank as a cashier. She again met McKinley, but by this time he was a successful attorney with a thriving practice in Canton and she was a beautiful young woman. For some reason he had to make daily deposits at the bank (along with a gift of flowers). The two also met on the sidewalk every Sunday on their way to church. He taught Sunday school at the Methodist Church and she did the same at the Presbyterian Church. They married in the new Presbyterian Church when she was 23 and he was 27. Her father gave them a house as a wedding present. Both the church and the house still stand.

The Saxton-McKinley House as it looks today

McKinley's devotion to Ida was celebrated in verse in this small book, A McKinley Romance.

William devoted himself to his business with the same determination that Ida applied to being a good wife, mother, and homemaker. But "happily ever after" is never guaranteed. Tragedy hit. Her mother and her five-month old daughter both died when Ida was only 26. By the time she was pregnant with her second daughter, she was seriously ill. In spite of failing health, Ida doted over her new baby with constant attention and obsessive concern, but this daughter died two years later when she was only three years old. Life crashed down around Ida, and she became epileptic, suffering from blinding headaches and convulsions.

McKinley was elected to Congress in 1876, and the McKinleys moved to Washington. They employed a full-time maid for Ida, but McKinley never left her for more than a few hours. When William was elected president, Ida insisted on attending all social functions, even traveling with McKinley on presidential business. The public never knew that Ida was an epileptic and the term was never used during her lifetime. She suffered a seizure at the Inaugural Ball, but that didn't deter her or discourage McKinley. She would receive White House guests while seated in a chair. She always held a small bouquet of flowers in her hands so that she appeared to be unable to shake hands. In addition, the McKinleys broke White House protocol by always seating Ida next to her husband. If she had a seizure during a state dinner, McKinley would calmly place a handkerchief over her face until the seizure passed. He never even interrupted his conversation. He had White House staff standing at the wall behind her chair, so that if the seizure were more than a handkerchief and a moment could mask, they would quietly carry her from the dining room until she could recover and return to the table without remark. While in the White House, the McKinleys entertained with musicales and Sunday evening hymn sings. Ida made many public appearances as First Lady, but her affliction caused embarrassment and tension for those around her. The only person who seemed to never be uncomfortable was devoted husband William McKinley. Although Ida was a jealous, petulant, demanding and possessive woman, McKinley always saw "the most beautiful girl he had ever met."

Ida spent her leisure time crocheting house slippers, literally thousands of pairs of house slippers, shipped to friends, relatives and charities. Many still exist.

When William McKinley was shot and killed at the beginning of his second term, it was also a near fatal shot for Ida. She lived another six years back in their first home in Canton, Ohio, where she sat in her private sitting room, crocheting in her rocking chair next to a table on which she kept a vase of fresh carnations. William had always worn a fresh carnation in his jacket lapel, and would reach up and touch it as a signal to her across a crowded room to say, "I love you."

Ida spent her leisure time crocheting house slippers, literally thousands of pairs of house slippers, shipped to friends, relatives and charities.

For Ida, life was a painful struggle. After losing her mother and daughters, she fought to keep her husband the only way she knew how, by demanding his total love and attention. He never faltered in giving it. He was saintly in his care and devotion. Even when he was shot and lay dying, he warned the staff to be careful how they told Ida, "Be very careful." for he worried about her reaction more than his own impending death. Although initially begging to die with William, Ida pulled herself together and participated in the funeral ceremonies. She had no reported seizures after McKinley's death, although she still remained an invalid. She willed herself to live long enough to oversee the building of the McKinley mausoleum. She died just four days before the dedication and was buried there with her beloved William and their two daughters.

Ida viewed God as a punishing God who took her children and afflicted her with illness because of some failure on her part. Rather than risk more errors, Ida simply withdrew into herself and waited for heaven.

Lessons from Ida

Yea, I have loved thee with an everlasting love (Jeremiah 31:3).

Cast thy burden upon the Lord, and he shall sustain thee: he shall never suffer the righteous to be moved (Psalms 55:22).

Cast me not off in the time of old age; forsake me not when my strength faileth (Psalms 71:9).

O God, be not far from me: O my God, make haste for my help (Psalms 71:12).

The world was too much with Ida. She was unable to respond because she saw God as her executioner instead of her savior. Her glass wasn't half-empty; she didn't even have a glass for God to fill. Since no one really understood epilepsy in the 1800s, perhaps Ida thought she was possessed of the devil or so full of sin that God couldn't save her. We don't know the reasons, but we do know that Ida went from a beautiful, talented young woman, attracting beaus in the bank, to a broken, lost soul. McKinley never failed her, but man alone couldn't save her.

Dear God, **thank You for Your saints and Your angels. Help us to sign on as trainees in providing Your healing touch to all we meet. Guide our eyes, our lips, our hands, and our feet that we may give love, not pity; care, not consternation; and joy, not judgment. Amen.**

26

Edith Kermit Carow Roosevelt

"Everything she did was for the happiness of others."
How Edie wanted to be remembered.

▨ *Meet Edie*

Born	Connecticut, 1861
Married	Theodore Roosevelt, 1886
Children	Six (one step-daughter, five children)
First Lady	1901-1909
Died	1948 at age 87
Edie's world	Construction on the Panama Canal begins; "Teddy Bears" are introduced (in honor of President Theodore Roosevelt); the United Methodist Church is founded; the first J.C. Penney opens; instant coffee is invented.

Edie, her seven children (she always counted Teddy as one of the kids), and a menagerie of pets charged into the White House and sent the staff scrambling for cover. Known as the "White House Gang," this brood put the old house to its first real test as a home.

The nation was also put to the test as it reeled from another death of a sitting president (William McKinley) and witnessed the swearing in of a war hero more known for his life as a cowboy than as a politician. But "Rough Rider" Teddy was a popular and successful president due in no small measure to his wife, Edie.

Edith Carow and Teddy grew up from infancy together in New York. He called her Edie. She called him Teedie. Both loved reading and sports. They had an "understanding," but the love story took a short detour. Teddy left for Harvard and Edie enrolled in a private school for girls in New York. Teddy met Alice Lee in Boston, fell in love and married her in 1880. However, only four years later, Teddy's wife and his mother both died in the family home on Valentine's Day, 1884. His mother died in the morning of typhoid fever and Alice died a few hours later while giving birth to their daughter, named Alice in her memory. Teddy ran out west to work off his grief on a cattle range and as a deputy sheriff.

Two years later, Teddy returned to New York and renewed his friendship with Edith Carow, and renewed a little more than that. They married in 1886. Teddy had built a huge home on Long Island, and Edie took over the chore of rearing her young stepdaughter Alice and managing a 26-room estate. Edie was a strict manager and the restraining force of the growing family even though she loved sports and animals as much as the rest. The house was soon booming with the addition of Teddy and Edie's five children: Theodore, Kermit, Ethel, Archibald, and Quentin.

When McKinley was felled by an assassin's bullet, Theodore Roosevelt became president of the United States and Edie became First Lady with stunning, sudden transition. She had to move her brood into the White House—not an easy task. Her first major job was to obtain approval for a complete renovation of the White House including the building of the "West Wing" to house the political and public offices, thereby allowing the "East Wing" to finally be a private residence. Prior to this time the public use to walk in on the First Family at any time.

Theodore Roosevelt, Jr., with macaw, Eli.

Edie also established the Ladies Picture Gallery and was the first First Lady to have a social secretary. This was not so much out of convenience as it was for the protection of her children. She tried to control the media's demands for pictures of her children by releasing pictures and stories on a regular basis. This didn't help curtail the stories of Alice, then a teenager, who created scandals to the point that her father had to remark, "I can be president of the United States or I can control Alice. I cannot possibly do both." He finally gave up on controlling "Princess Alice" and married her off in a popular White House wedding.

Edie was a gracious and popular First Lady, creating entertaining musicales, and starting a "cabinet wives" luncheon. However, less time was spent in dining than was spent in passing moral judgment over other men in the government. Edie opposed any man thought to be a womanizer. Her other time was spent in trying to control the antics of the "White House Gang," which included such pranks as a horse in the elevator and snakes in the pantry.

After their tenure in the White House, the Roosevelts retired back on Long Island in 1909. Teddy died of a blood clot in 1919 at age 60. Edie survived Teddy by almost 30 years and spent those years traveling around the world, working for charities and for the

Republican Party. In 1927, Edie wrote about being an empty nester, long before the term became so popular.

> *"Women who marry pass their best and happiest years in giving life and fostering it, meeting and facing the problems of the next generation and helping the universe to move, and those born with the wander-foot are sometimes a bit irked by the weight of the always beloved shackles. Then the birds fly, the nest is empty, and at the feet of the knitters in the sun lies the wide world."*
>
> Edith Roosevelt, "The Odyssey of a Grandmother"

Edie was an independent woman even in her religion. She and the children attended the Episcopal Church while Teddy went to the Dutch Reformed Church. She supported higher education and suffrage for women, but her main and compelling love was her husband and family.

Lessons from Edie

Every wise woman buildeth her house: but the foolish plucketh it down with her hands (Proverbs 14:1).

Verily I say until you, Except ye be converted, and become as little children, ye shall not enter into the kingdom of heaven (Matthew 18:3).

From Edie we learn mothering skills from a master: control with kindness, not wrath. Edie managed her house and family with more humor and understanding than with punishment. While some complained that the children were unruly, her family seemed to succeed, where many previous sons and daughters of the White

House failed miserably. She never lost her spirit of adventure or her joy for living. Devotion to God, duty to country, and dedication to her husband and family all combined to make Edie a remarkable wife and mother.

Dear God, **grant us patience. Grant us wisdom, that we may know when to let go and when to hold tight. And, no matter how hard the world gets, help us to keep joy in tact, so that we can become and remain as little children for You, in Your service and to Your pleasure. Amen.**

27

Helen (Nellie) Herron Taft

The White House was her life-long dream.

▦ *Meet Nellie*

Born	Ohio, 1861
Married	William Taft, 1886
Children	Three (two sons and one daughter)
First Lady	1909-1913
Died	1943 at age 82
Nellie's World	Personal Income Tax begins; *Gideon Bibles* placed in hotels; the Titanic sinks; Oreo cookies appear on store shelves.

Wide-eyed and tongue-tied, seventeen-year-old Nellie Herron stared at the opulence of the White House and declared that she was looking at her future home. It was at that impressionable age that Nellie was invited to the White House to meet First Lady, Lucy Hayes, a friend of the family. Nellie gaped at the chandeliers and portraits, and set her dream in motion. All she had to do was find a husband who would be president.

Nellie met William Taft at a party the following year, but she wasn't sure he was her presidential prospect. They dated others and each worked for seven years before Will's persistence paid off and Nellie agreed to marry him. They settled in Cincinnati, and Will was appointed to the Superior Court of Ohio when he was only 29. He was thrilled because his lifelong dream was to be a Supreme Court Justice. Nellie was not thrilled with anything short of a president, but bided her time until he was appointed Solicitor General of the United States. This appointment took them to Washington, which fit in with Nellie's grand plans. This appointment was short-lived, and they returned to Cincinnati where Will served as a Federal Circuit Court judge for eight years.

Then in 1900, President McKinley sent the Tafts to the Philippines to help establish a civil government. They stayed four years, and Taft became the first civil governor-general of the

Nellie Taft with the President in her automobile. Nellie insisted on having a fleet of automobiles for the family's use, instead of the old-fashioned horse and carriage.

Nellie Taft (right) in front of police at the 1912 Democratic convention. Republican Nellie Taft remains the only First Lady to have attended the opposition party's convention.

Islands. Taft had a chance for a Supreme Court appointment, but turned it down much to Nellie's delight. While serving as Secretary of War, Taft gained national attention . . . and five years later was elected president of the United States. It took over 30 years, but Nellie's dream finally came true. She triumphantly rode in the carriage with her husband to the Inauguration, the first wife to do so.

Nervous Nellie, as she was quickly labeled, tried to do everything. It had taken her 30 years to get to the White House, and she wasn't going to miss a second. Her micro-management drove the staff crazy. She insisted in being involved in all of her husband's conferences and receptions. She was a "take charge" lady who frequently forgot who in the family was the actual president of the United States. She interceded on behalf of a small child who was refused admittance to the US by immigration officials because he was believed to be "an idiot." A week later his mother sent a letter of thanks, explaining that he was merely "tongue tied." She interceded in the hanging of an African American man.

Her obsessive behavior led to a serious stroke from which she recovered after more than 18 months. She didn't mind missing the social functions. In fact she thought them trivial. But she sorely missed the cabinet meetings. Taft, although he did well as president, did not share her dream and once remarked that the White House was "the loneliest place in the world." They worked as political partners, but they didn't agree on many issues. She liked to smoke and drink; he supported prohibition. Taft finally agreed to support suffrage, but Nellie refused. Taft was easy-going and jovial; Nellie was intense and out-spoken. They were the first White House couple to use a car and the last to have a cow.

When Nellie requested a car, she was told that she would have to settle for a Ford, because the transportation budget could not afford the Pierce-Arrows that she wanted. She managed to get a discount from Pierce-Arrow by allowing them to advertise that they supplied cars to the White House. She didn't blink at commercial exploitation as long as she got what she wanted.

After leaving the White House, they moved to Connecticut, where Taft accepted a professorship at Yale. Eight years later, Taft finally achieved his lifelong dream. He was appointed Chief Justice of the Supreme Court. He retired after eight years due to ill health and died in 1930 at the age of 72. Nellie requested that he be buried in Arlington National Cemetery, the first president to be buried there. Nellie survived another 13 years and was also buried at Arlington. It was fitting that her dream began and ended in Washington.

We know a little about Nellie's faith from her writings and those of others. Nellie was a practicing Episcopalian and meticulous about going to church every Sunday, but was not a particularly spiritual person. She did leave one very lasting impression on Washington. At her request, 3,000 cherry trees were imported from Japan, and she planted the first one in 1912. Thanks to Nellie, springtime is a beautiful time in Washington.

She writes of a trip to Rome and a visit to the Pope in her autobiography, *Recollection of Full Years*:

> *I was educated in the strictest Presbyterianism, while my husband's mother was a Unitarian, and Puritan in her training and in all her instincts. We could not help feeling that we had been led into a prominent position in a strange environment. But, unshaken though we were in our religious affiliations, we appreciated the real beauty of the ceremonies and knew that we should rejoice in the unusual privilege accorded us which would never be ours again.*

Lessons from Nellie

Now faith is the substance of things hoped for, the evidence of things not seen (Hebrews 11:1).

Hear my prayer, O God; give ear to the words of my mouth (Psalm 54:2).

Nervous Nellie's lessons are good ones. From Nellie we learn to be careful what we pray for; we just might get it. All her life Nellie wanted to be First Lady. Glitter, glamour, power and fame had been etched into her teenage mind. She saw none of the troubles, the heartache, or the stresses of the job until she entered the White House and her dream became a nightmare. In her ambition, she sacrificed the career ambitions and aspirations of her husband, and ruined her own health. But God is merciful. He granted Nellie a second chance. She recovered from her stroke. And when she refocused her attention on the things of life that were truly important and supported her husband in his true calling, he, too, was finally able to fulfill his dream. They both won.

Dear God, let it be Your will, not mine, this day and all days of my life. Amen.

28 a

Ellen Louise Axson Wilson

"...entirely too much inclined to make her own decisions."
Ellen's father

Meet Ellen

Born	Georgia, 1860
Married	Woodrow Wilson, 1885
Children	Three daughters
First Lady	1913-1914
Died	1914 at the age of 54
Ellen's World	World War breaks out in Europe (would later be called World War I); the Panama Canal is completed.

Ellen Axson and Woodrow Wilson met in church. Where else would the offspring of two Presbyterian ministers be on a Sunday morning? Charming, intelligent, and gifted, Ellen obviously appealed to the equally charming, handsome and academic Woodrow Wilson. He proposed five months after meeting her, but Ellen demurred for two years while she cared for her ill father and attended art school in New York City, and Woodrow studied at John Hopkins University. After they married in 1885, Wilson taught at Bryn Mawr, Wesleyan College and Princeton. (Wilson was the first and only president of the United States with a Ph.D.) He became president of Princeton in 1902. After only one elected office, governor of New Jersey, Wilson was nominated and elected president of the United States.

Along the way, the Wilsons had three daughters: Margaret, Jessie, and Eleanor.

Ellen entered the White House with the same good nature and efficiency with which she tackled every job, but she never really liked being First Lady. In a thank you note to President Taft, she remarked, "I am naturally the most unambitious of women, and life in the White House has no attractions for me." But she was good at it. She had gleaned valuable experience and considerable grace from two years as the wife of the governor of New Jersey.

When the responsibilities of being First Lady became burdensome, she retreated to the art studio with a skylight that she had built on the third floor of the White House and painted. She donated many of her paintings to charity, and art historians note that she was "not bad." She was Wilson's sounding board and helped with his speeches and served as his advisor. She was an activist in her own right. Appalled by the slums in Washington and driven as the descendent of slave owners, she lobbied to get a bill passed to improve housing conditions for African Americans living in poverty.

Ellen's determination to pursue a career as a professional artist earned her the nickname, "Ellie the Man-Hater." Some of her paintings are shown here in the background.

Ellen lived to see two of her daughters married in the White House, but she died shortly after the second wedding in 1914 of Blight's disease. Her last words were, "... take good care of my husband." Her funeral was held in the same church in Rome, Georgia where she had met Woodrow 31 years earlier.

Ellen was a Presbyterian and provided religious instruction to her daughters. She served on the Board of Associated Charities and maintained a self-sacrificing commitment to her community and country. Even while in art school in New York, she volunteered two nights a week at a missionary school. Although a supporter of suffrage, she did not take a public stand on the issue. When rumors arose that Woodrow was seeing and corresponding with other women, Ellen refused to display any jealousy, and instead, invited the women to events as friends of the family. Ellen always took the high road. Although she did not ignore her own talents, she was first and foremost the helpmate of her husband, and a caring, devoted role model for her daughters.

Lessons from Ellen

Jesus said unto him, If thou wilt be perfect, go and sell that thou hast, and give to the poor, and thou shalt have treasure in heaven: come and follow me (Matthew 19:21).

From Ellen we learn to look for the rainbow, not the storm clouds. Ellen always looked for a solution, not a situation. She developed her own talents, but used them almost exclusively for the benefits of others. She turned potential conflicts into friendships. She recognized weaknesses, but worked to heal them instead of excising them. No matter how reluctant she might have been, Ellen did what she had to do for the greater good of her husband, family, and country. She understood duty and responsibility above self. But her crowning achievement was her ability to forgive. Inviting the women with whom her husband was reportedly seeing was forgiveness in action. Her steadfast support for her husband, her refusal to publicly embarrass him, and her stepping between truth and perception to protect him are admirable.

Dear God, **open our hearts and our minds, that we will give unconditionally of our love, never asking what we will receive in return. Help us realize that the giving is our gift. Amen.**

28 b

Edith Bolling Galt Wilson

"Ready to follow the road where love leads."

Meet Edith

Born	Virginia, 1872
Married	Norman Galt, 1896
	Woodrow Wilson, 1915
Children	None
First Lady	1915-1921
Died	1961 at age 89
Edith's World	World War I erupts and involves the United States; Prohibition is enacted; Daylight Saving Time is initiated.

President Woodrow Wilson, newly widowed and severely depressed, ran into pretty Edith Galt on the White House steps. She, too, was widowed. He immediately invited her to tea. Wilson soon began calling and going for rides and walks with Edith. He was unaccustomed to functioning alone, and needed a woman by his side. Edith seemed to fit the bill nicely. He installed a private phone line between the White House and Edith's home, and although he knew it was not politically correct, he convinced Edith to marry him less than a year after the death of his wife, Ellen. He knew it would appear to be too soon, but he said that "in this place time is not measured by weeks, or months, or years, but by deep human experience." He even confessed to past love affairs and warned her that his past and her life would be assaulted in his reelection bid. It didn't matter; they were two lonely people and it was a true love match.

Edith's first husband had died in 1908 and she had managed herself and the family jewelry business for seven years. She traveled and entertained extensively and was a noted figure in Washington society. Edith was the first woman in Washington to have an electric car, and she loved to golf and play pool. When she entered the White House, she brought energy and entertainment, and served as Wilson's personal assistant in all of his functions. In fact, she never left his side, working with him at his desk every

Grazing flocks of sheep cropped the White House lawn during the Wilson years, releasing men for the war effort during World War I.

Edith assists her husband.

afternoon and evening. The social aspects of the duties of First Ladies who preceded her were abandoned in the grim reality of the United States engaged in World War I. There were simply more important issues to address than state dinners, teas, and balls. Edith stepped up. She set an example for the war effort by sewing shirts and bandages for the Red Cross, observing meatless days, and even bringing a herd of sheep to maintain the White House lawn. The wool from the sheep was auctioned off for the Red Cross and Salvation Army.

Despite Edith's best efforts in supporting her husband, Wilson suffered a severe stroke in October, 1919. Edith took over his care and no one else had access to the president except his personal physician for several weeks. Critics said that Edith had become the acting president and assumed powers she had no right to exercise. She was called "Presidentress," "Her Regency," the "Secret President," and worse. Supporters claim she saved the president's life by protecting him from further stress. Whatever the exact circumstances or length of time, Edith did screen all of his visitors and mail and acted as his intermediary for several weeks or months. Woodrow Wilson never fully recovered and died three years after leaving the White House. Edith was only 51 at his death and survived him by almost 38 years.

We know very little about her faith, but what we do know is oddly contradictory. Edith was a devotee of astrology, but also had a pew in St. Margaret's Episcopal Church.

Lesson's from Edith

We looked for peace, but none came, and for a time of health, and behold trouble! (Jeremiah 9:15)

True healing demands changes. Edith knew that her critically ill husband could not recover without removing him from the stresses and pressures that brought on his stroke. She stood her ground, literally, and barred all visitors to his private chambers in the White House. With her continual care and under her protection, Wilson slowly recovered and resumed most of his duties. In spite of harsh criticism and suspicion, Edith did what she had to do, what she knew was right. She took over routine duties and details, and selected specific matters for her husband to address. She knew when to step forward and she knew when to step back. And she did it in the name of love. This is being the ultimate helpmeet.

Dear God, grant us health, for with a healthy body all things are possible. Grant us gratitude, that we may always know that our health comes from You. And give us courage to use our bodies to Your glory without regard for the judgement of fellow humans. Amen.

29

Florence Kling Harding

"The happy wife is not necessarily the one who's married to the best man on earth, but the one who's philosophical enough to make the best of what she's got." Flo Harding "The Duchess"

Meet Florence

Born	Ohio, 1860
Married	Henry DeWolfe, 1880
	Warren G. Harding, 1891
Children	One by DeWolfe
First Lady	1921-1923
Died	1924 at age 64
Florence's World	Prohibition rules the nation; *Readers Digest* is published; the lie detector and the bulldozer are invented.

Florence Harding has the dubious distinction of being the only First Lady accused of poisoning her husband. Rumors were fueled by speculation when the physician who treated him (a potential witness!) died shortly thereafter of the same symptoms. There was never any credible evidence to support the rumors (or any formal inquiry, for that matter), but it was well known that the Hardings didn't have a happy marriage, and his death did occur right before the public was to learn of some nasty scandals within his administration. The timing was unfortunate.

Florence and Warren both lived in the small town of Marion, Ohio where Warren was trying to run a weekly newspaper. Florence was from the wealthiest family in town, but she had eloped when young and her father had disowned her. Her first husband abandoned her and her young son, and Florence turned to teaching piano lessons to support herself. She met Warren in 1890 and quickly took control of the handsome, but weak newspaperman. She turned his failing newspaper around while he turned his attention to politics. He had the look and voice of a statesman and quickly rose from state office, to the Senate, to the presidency. She was a tireless, talented worker on his political campaigns. Owning a newspaper didn't hurt. He called her "the Duchess." And she said of him, "I have only one real hobby—my husband."

Florence was 61 when they entered the White House, but she embraced the job of First Lady with the zeal and energy of a much younger woman. She opened the White House to everyone and had continuous parties. But their quest for popularity came at a high price: their integrity. Both Warren and Florence were influenced and used by their "friends" and quickly found themselves in the midst of scandals and corruption. Just two years into the administration, the Hardings decided to take a trip to the West Coast in an attempt to regain confidence from the public. In California, Harding died suddenly of a blood clot. Florence, herself suffering from a diseased kidney, died less than two years later.

Florence and Warren claimed to be just plain folks who wanted to be popular. The country loved them the first year, but people soon learned that there was no substance behind the public images. It was as if the country was being led by two cardboard images, manipulated from behind by unscrupulous and greedy political appointees and associates. Harding loved his poker parties and women, but never grasped the importance of his position. (Remember, he had trouble running a small newspaper.) Florence knew her husband was having affairs and tried unsuccessfully to keep him in the White House, but her efforts only created more distance and disdain from her husband. Harding, although he was a terrible husband, credited Florence with his political success saying, "I couldn't have done it without the Duchess," but also chafed at her controlling nature, "She wants to be the drum major in every band that passes."

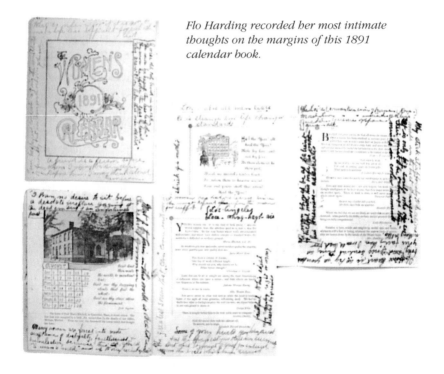

Flo Harding recorded her most intimate thoughts on the margins of this 1891 calendar book.

We know little about Florence's faith. She was a Methodist and tried to take Warren to church as often as she could. She supported charities and women's and animal causes, but her true heart was in the hospitals. She spent hundreds of hours in the veterans' hospitals visiting the soldiers. They loved her and her hats. She returned on a regular basis because it was the one place she found happiness and acceptance, and felt she could be truly useful.

Lessons from Florence

Faithful are the wounds of a friend, but the kisses of an enemy are deceitful (Proverbs 27:6).

It is better to dwell in a corner of the housetop than with a brawling woman in a wide house (Proverbs 21:9).

The White House was a wide house, but not wide enough for Warren and Florence to live in harmony. Florence was determined that Warren would be president regardless of how he thought about it. He thought it was a good idea as long as he didn't have to work too hard or give up his friends, alcohol (during prohibition!), women, and poker. Warren had the looks and the smooth, deep voice of a politician, and it was the first presidential election in which women had the right to vote. Alas, a handsome face swayed inexperienced women voters. Florence and Warren did not have bad intentions, but they were not cautious or skilled enough to control those around them who did. Harding rightly lamented in his first year in office that he wasn't worried about his enemies; it was his friends that would be his downfall. Lessons to be learned? High jobs and big houses still don't guarantee successful careers or happy marriages. Listening to the wrong voices can be disastrous.

Dear God, give us penetrating wisdom, eyes that see beyond the clothes, ears that hear behind the words, hands that can discern a caring touch from a grasping hold. Guide us to find Your face, Your voice, and Your hand amidst the din and rubble. Amen.

30

Grace Goodhue Coolidge

"Being wife to a government worker is a very confining position."
Grace Coolidge while in the White House

Meet Grace

Born	Vermont, 1879
Married	Calvin Coolidge, 1905
Children	Two sons (one died at age 16)
First Lady	1923-1929
Died	1957 at age 78
Grace's World	Cecil B. DeMille's film, *The Ten Commandments*, is released; the dance, the Charleston, is the rage; Wheaties and Mickey Mouse debut.

You have to love a woman who owned a pet raccoon (named Rebecca), and Grace was a lovely woman. She was lively and witty, loved to socialize and dance, and was the exact opposite of her dour, conservative husband, Silent Cal.

Grace was a teacher in a school for the deaf when she met Calvin. She was watering plants outside the school when she saw a man standing in a window of a neighboring house. He was shaving in his long underwear and had a hat on his head. She laughed so loudly that he heard her, glanced out the window, turned, and resumed shaving. Perhaps it was her laughter that attracted him. We'll never know for sure, but Calvin arranged to meet her. Two years later, in spite of opposite personalities, they married. They had two sons.

Cal was elected to the House and the Senate, and served as Governor of Massachusetts before getting the vice presidential nomination and winning on the ticket with Warren G. Harding in 1920. Grace was Cal's vote-winner, the family diplomat, and the perfect symbol for the roaring twenties. Neither of them was prepared for Calvin Coolidge to become President of the United States, but when President Harding died suddenly from a heart

Grace Coolidge at a baseball game.

attack, Cal stepped into the Oval
Office. For the fifth time in the
country's short history, a president
died in office and the vice-
president was called into duty for a
job for which he had no
experience or training. (As a matter
of historical record, Cal did fine.)

Grace was a graduate of the
University of Vermont and
continued with her sorority,
Pi Beta Phi, most of her life.
Her passions included children,
pets, baseball, and music. She did
not get involved in politics, and
Calvin forbade her to give any
interviews. He also forbade her to
dance, drive, fly in an airplane,
wear culottes, or have her hair
curled. He had a long list of
things he didn't like, and one
thing that he did: he liked to see
her in beautiful dresses. Evidently
he had quite a lot to say about
her wardrobe. While First Lady Grace was posing for her official
portrait, she had on a stunning red dress. Her white collie, Rob
Roy, was posed beside her. When Coolidge saw the scenario, he
said her white dress would be better. The portrait painter explained
that he needed contrast since the dog was white. "No problem,"
Coolidge reportedly replied, "Just paint the dog red."

Grace accepted all of her husband's restrictions with her usual
sunny disposition, but when she was upset, she knitted. With Silent
Cal, her needles had to be clicking almost all the time.

Cal was reelected in 1924, but declined a second full term. He died four years after leaving the White House. Grace lived another 24 years.

Grace was a deeply religious person. She joined the Congregational Church when she was sixteen. Her father was known as the "handy deacon" in the church because he knew how to repair the organ. Her faith is best expressed in *The Open Door*, the poem she wrote after the tragic death of their 16 year-old son. She was able to work through his death, but for Silent Cal, their son's death made him even more recalcitrant and distant than ever. Grace, on the other hand, put her grief into action. She demonstrated her faith daily in her dedication to the welfare of children and the disabled. She worked with the Children's Hospital, the Camp Fire Girls, the Girl Scouts, and Christmas Seals. She continued to raise funds for the Clarke Institute for the Deaf in Vermont and also for the Red Cross. She was known as "Sunshine" by the White House staff—a very fitting title, almost as fitting as "Grace."

Lessons from Grace

Whoso findeth a wife findeth a good thing, and obtaineth favour of the Lord (Proverbs 18:22).

By whom also we have access by faith into this grace wherein we stand, and rejoice in hope of the glory of God. And not only so, but we glory in tribulations also: knowing that tribulation worketh patience . . . (Romans 5:2-3).

God doesn't save us from tribulations. He never promised us a problem-free life. But what is it worth to have an all-knowing and all-powerful friend who will walk with us and sit with us and cry with us? Priceless. Grace knew the presence of God. He was with her even through the death of her son and her grieving. Grace says it best in this poem.

The Open Door

"You, my son,
Have shown me God.
Your kiss upon my cheek
Has made me feel the gentle touch
Of Him who leads us on.
The memory of your smile, when young,
Reveals His face,
As mellowing years come on apace.
And when you went before,
You left the gates of Heaven ajar
That I might glimpse,
Approaching from afar,
The glories of His grace.
Hold, son, my hand,
Guide me along the path,
That, coming,
I may stumble not
Nor roam,
Nor fail to show the way
Which leads us – Home."

– Grace Coolidge, Five years after the tragic death of their
16-year-old son

31

Lou Henry Hoover

*"It isn't so important what others think of you as
what you feel inside."* Lou Hoover

Meet Mary

Born	Iowa, 1874
Married	Herbert Hoover, 1899
Children	Two sons
First Lady	1929-1933
Died	1944 at age 69
Lou's World	The Stock Market crashes; Prohibition is repealed; Bisquick is developed; the Blondie comic strip is introduced.

Lou Hoover could do anything and had the education, experience, and energy to get it done. Lou was the first female to graduate from Stanford with a degree in geology. She met her future husband Herbert in a geology lab at Stanford in 1894 when she was a freshman and he was a senior. When she graduated in 1898, Herbert was already working in Australia, but sent her a marriage proposal by telegram. She must have replied in the affirmative for they were married the next year and she went with him to China. He was a mining engineer who managed and owned mining firms and became a self-made millionaire.

Herbert's mines took them all over the world. While overseas, Lou learned to speak Chinese, French and German. She would speak to Herbert in Mandarin if she didn't want others to understand her. They went from the Boxer Rebellion in China to the First World War in London. They coordinated relief efforts in Great Britain and Belgium and traveled across the United Sates collecting donations of food, clothing and money. Hoover was appointed head of the US Food Administration in 1917 and Secretary of Commerce in 1921. Before running for President, Hoover had never held an elected office. Hoover ran on the platform of a chicken in every pot, but the chicken flew the coop with the stock market crash and the onset of the Great Depression.

In 1898, Lou Henry, shown here in her classroom at Stanford, became possibly the first woman to graduate with a degree in geology.

The Hoovers entered the White House and made many changes in style and customs. The entertained daily with dozens of last-minute guests much to the dismay of the staff. Lou renovated the public rooms using most of their own furniture. Since it was the Depression, they paid the staff and many of the renovations out of their own private funds and Hoover donated his entire salary to charity.

Herbert was a Quaker, and Lou adopted many of the Quaker beliefs, however she remained an Episcopalian. Greatly affected by the suffering of the unemployed during the Depression, Lou donated generously to social causes and actively campaigned for others to do the same. She was a girl scout leader and became their national president in 1922. She was

"Good women elect bad men by staying away from the polls."
Lou Hoover

also named Vice-president of the National Amateur Athletic Association, the first woman to hold office in that association. Lou supported prohibition (she even did away with Hoover's wine collection) and integration. When she invited a black woman to tea in the White House, she received scalding press from the southern newspapers. But Hoover backed her up and invited a black professor to lunch the next week. Undaunted, Lou invited the Tuskegee Institute choir to sing in the White House. But the Great Depression was too much for any one couple. They were ridiculed and defiled by the media and Hoover suffered a humiliating defeat by Roosevelt.

After leaving the White House in 1933, Hoover ran unsuccessfully for reelection and Lou continued by his side knowing that he was a great man that history would vindicate someday. She did not live to see that vindication. She died suddenly of a heart attack in 1944.

We know Lou's faith and spirit from her actions, not her words. She anonymously supported individuals, families and charities throughout her life. When she discovered that the mountain retreat they had built outside of Washington had no school in the area, she built and paid for one. Upon her death, Hoover discovered hundreds of people Lou had aided privately with no one's knowledge except herself. Although not given to outward religious expression, Lou certainly practiced the Golden Rule and was generous with her time and tithes.

This letter, written by Lou to her two young sons, was in her personal papers. She wrote it just before World War I in case she didn't make it home to them.

"I know that if I should die, I can pray my soul to go over to my two dear little boys and to help and comfort their souls. Of course you can't see it or hear it. But sometimes you will know that I am there, because your own little soul inside you will feel nice and comfy and cozy, because my bigger, older one is cuddling it. And when you are in trouble, and call for me to come to help you, and pray God to give you more force, why I can come right to you and bring along the new force he is sending to you."

Lessons from Lou

Be not forgetful to entertain strangers: for thereby some have entertained angels unawares (Hebrews 13:2).

Take heed that ye do not your alms before men, to be seen of them: otherwise ye have no reward of your Father which is in heaven (Matthew 6:1).

... Verily I say unto you, Inasmuch as ye have done it unto one of the least of these my brethren, ye have done it unto me (Matthew 25:40).

From Lou we learn charity and tolerance. For Lou and Herb it was the classic case of being in the wrong place at the wrong time. The country and the world were on the verge of economic disaster before Hoover was ever nominated. When the stock market crashed, abuse was piled on the president. Although it took a heavy toll on both of them (12 million people were unemployed in 1932), Lou remarked "Bert can take it better than most people because he has deeply engrained in him the Quaker feeling that nothing matters if you are right with God." Although there was little that two people could do, even as president and First Lady, they personally worked and contributed as much as was humanly possible. They directly challenged the segregationists of the day by inviting racial minorities to the White House, and became great, but private philanthropists. Lou was so diligent in keeping her gifts secret that it worked against her. If the public knew the millions they were spending out of their own funds for the staff, the White House, and hundreds of individuals and charities, perhaps the abuse would have quieted. But Lou and Bert were not doing it to please the press or the public. They were working to please God.

Dear God, Help me to understand that it is just between You and me. What I do or not do, give or not give, I answer to You. I need no resume, no awards or trophies. You will know, and that is the highest reward. Amen.

32

❦

Anna Eleanor Roosevelt Roosevelt

"Adapting one's plans to the needs of others is what makes life worth living." Eleanor Roosevelt

Meet Eleanor

Born	New York, 1884
Married	Franklin D. Roosevelt, 1905
Children	Six (one died in infancy)
First Lady	1933-1945
Died	1962 at age 78
Eleanor's World	The Great Depression; Social Security Act passes; World War II rages; Golden Gate Bridge is completed; the Hindenburg explodes.

Eleanor never walked anywhere; she ran. Her son described her as "a sort of roving one-woman task force for social reform and international good will." Accolades do not do the lady justice. She is routinely referred to as our greatest First Lady and frequently labeled "First Lady of the World." But her greatness did not come quickly or without heartache.

Eleanor was the daughter of Anna Hall and Elliott Roosevelt, younger brother of Theodore. But she was orphaned by age 10 and was reared by a stern great aunt and tutors. She was taught at home and at a boarding school in London, but at 18, her grandmother declared that she had enough education, and summoned her back to New York for her debut. A debut was the last thing Eleanor wanted. She considered herself an "ugly duckling" and dreaded the social scene.

"No one can make you feel inferior without your consent."
Eleanor Roosevelt

But her return to New York had its reward. She ran into her distant cousin Franklin and they began dating. But Franklin's disapproving mother Sara had other plans for her son, and tried to keep Franklin home and away from all women. He persisted and in 1905 he and Eleanor were married. Eleanor was given away by none other than her uncle, Teddy Roosevelt, the president of the United States. Insecure and shy, Eleanor dreaded contacts with her mother-in-law and even the servants. It wasn't until Franklin entered politics and they moved away from his overbearing mother, that Eleanor began to be her own person.

Even before Franklin served in the New York Senate and as Assistant Secretary of the Navy in Washington, Eleanor began her lifelong career as helpmate. Her strength and support would prove invaluable when Franklin contacted polio in 1921. Eleanor faced the daunting task of rearing five children, supporting her husband's

Eleanor helped plan and fund an experimental housing development for families of coal miners in West Virginia.

political ambitions, and serving as his eyes, ears and legs. She taught school, inspected prisons, and opened a furniture business. She even became active in the State Democratic Committee to keep his interest in politics kindled. When he made a bid for governor, she forced herself to make public appearances and speeches, campaign, and visit the world over.

When Franklin was elected president, no First Lady had ever understood social conditions so well. Moving into the White House in 1933, her energy expanded, leaving people panting on the sidelines as she rushed down the steps and streets of Washington. Eleanor was the first First Lady to fly in a plane and jaunted everywhere to view farms, mines, schools, and soldiers. She wrote a daily newspaper column, broadcast regularly on the radio, and gave lectures whenever and wherever invited. Her hands were never still. In the middle of a conference, she would pull out her knitting and start clicking.

During World War II, Eleanor campaigned for the war effort and worried along with thousands of other mothers when all four of her sons went off to serve in the military. She visited the war hospitals and wrote hundreds of letters home to parents and spouses, praising the brave soldiers.

She advised Franklin on matters he requested and on matters she thought he should request. If a deserving person could not get an immediate appointment with the president, she would invite the person to lunch or dinner and then ask pointed questions across the table and over the broccoli until the President got the message. She adopted dozens of causes and worked tirelessly on all of them. She fought for programs for farm assistance, women's rights, March of Dimes for polio research, and racial equality. She was so adamant about equality that she resigned from the Daughters of the American Revolution because of their racial policies.

Although Eleanor fought and won battles all over the world, she lost her first and most painful battle on the home front. Early in their marriage, fifteen years before they entered the White House, Eleanor discovered that Franklin was having an affair with her own social secretary. Outraged, but realistic, Eleanor agreed not to seek a divorce for the sake of Franklin's career. However, from 1918 until he died in 1945, they never lived as man and wife, and rarely even spent time alone together. Even years later, when FDR was ill and reached out for some assistance or comfort, Eleanor drew away. She could not forgive.

Mrs. Roosevelt rides with Britains's Queen Elizabeth, wife of George IV.

Although Eleanor served longer than any other First Lady, her efforts did not end with the death of her husband in 1945. The very next year she was appointed as a delegate to the new United Nations and helped write the Universal Declaration of Human Rights. She continued writing and fighting for equality until her death in 1962. The flags at the Capitol were lowered to half-mast upon her death, the first presidential widow so honored.

Eleanor was a Presbyterian and lived the Golden Rule throughout her life. For her, religion was ecumenical and required a broad, international acceptance. "I sometimes think that the same spirit pervades the good people in all religions. If you want others to respect your beliefs, you must in return give respect for theirs." When asked if she believed in an afterlife she answered in her usual pragmatic manner, "It always seemed to me that there must be some kind of immortality, because it would be such a wasted performance otherwise." Eleanor worked harder and longer than any other woman for equal rights, fair wages, youth programs, and hundreds of other worthwhile programs and issues. Perhaps it was too much to ask for her to be also a forgiving wife.

Lessons from Eleanor

For as the body without the spirit is dead, so faith without works is also dead (James 2:26).

Through idleness of the hands the house droppeth through (Ecclesiastes 10:18).

And be kind to one another, tenderhearted, forgiving one another, even as God for Christ's sake has forgiven you (Ephesians 4:32).

From Eleanor we learn energy and commitment. There is much good work to do, and so little time on earth in which to do it. Eleanor took her dedication to good works to the extreme, sometimes antagonizing the very people she needed as allies. But her heart was pure. She was without prejudice. Unemployed miners, abandoned youth, African Americans, and Jews—all were worthy of her time and effort. Idleness was a sin to Eleanor.

But the other lesson we learn from Eleanor is that the inability to forgive is selfish and costly. Because she couldn't get past Franklin's indiscretions, she robbed herself of the possibility of a fulfilling family life (something that she was denied in youth when her parents died). And she also robbed Franklin of a chance to redeem himself. Later in life, when he really needed her friendship, she kept it withdrawn. Both spouses lost ... and no doubt their children suffered. Had she been able to soften her heart just a little, she could have had a family intact, and he could have known the unconditional love and forgiveness of Christ made manifest in the tender heart of his wife. It might have made all the difference in his being able to better govern his own behavior and be more pleasing to God.

Dear God, **direct our hearts, our hands, our feet, and our energy to further Your kingdom on earth, that people will know we are Christians by our deeds, not just our words. And please help us to be soft, to understand that service to You is more than action; it's living with an open heart. Amen.**

33

Elizabeth (Bess) Virginia Wallace Truman

"A woman's place in public is to sit beside her husband, be silent and be sure her hat is on straight." Bess Truman

Meet Bess

Born	Missouri, 1885
Married	Harry S. Truman, 1919
Children	one daughter
First Lady	1945-1953
Died	1982 at the age of 97!
Bess's world	World War II ends; Korean War starts; Dead Sea Scrolls unearthed; cake mixes and aluminum foil introduced.

People in Missouri are known for taking things slowly and deliberately. That might help explain the fact that Bess and Harry knew each other for 29 years and had several hundred dates before Bess finally said, "Yes." Harry and Bess first met in the Presbyterian Sunday school in Independence, Missouri. She was five and he was six. She was the belle of the town and he was a poor farm boy. But Harry never gave up loving and pursuing her ... and when she was 34 and he 35, they finally married. They moved into her mother's house in Independence, and Harry began a political career. He served in the Senate for ten years and in 1944 was elected vice president under Roosevelt. Unfortunately, for the sixth time in American history, a sitting president died in office, and the vice president and his family were transformed overnight from relatively unknown people to the newsmakers of the country.

Bess was 60 when she entered the White House and wanted nothing to do with the press or Washington society. The "Three Musketeers," as the staff called Harry, Bess, and their daughter Margaret, preferred quiet family evenings to any elaborate entertaining. Bess loved to play bridge and initiated a Spanish class in the White House, but they never learned any Spanish and she

Bess Truman christens an airplane.

never adopted a cause. Her cause was Harry. She spent most of her life trying to get him to stop swearing. When one aide complained that Truman had used the word "manure " in an interview, Bess replied that it was an improvement over what he usually said and to not complain. Her favorite and most frequent phrase was, "Harry, you shouldn't have said that." His favorite response: "Yes, Boss"

Harry discussed every issue with Bess. In every way she was his partner, albeit a silent partner. She shunned the spotlight, declined interviews and canceled the

During the Truman administration, the White House had to be gutted to the outside walls and rebuilt.

only press conference she ever scheduled. And it was probably a good thing that Harry had her undivided attention, because for him, the pressures of the presidency were immense. Under his administration, the United States decided to end World War II by dropping two atomic bombs on Japan, the Cold War was in full force, and the Korean War broke out. It was a challenging, dangerous time for the country.

It was also apparently challenging and dangerous living in the White House. The Trumans had to move from the White House to Blair House in 1948 when a ceiling caved in. The story goes that a piano leg crashed from the second floor through the first floor ceiling. An architect remarked that the White House was standing only because of habit and the whole structure was on the verge of collapse. Bess lobbied to keep the original structure, rather than build a new complex. The whole house was gutted to the outside walls and rebuilt. When they returned in 1952, it was a palace with 132 rooms and 20 baths.

They left the White House in 1953, and returned to a hero's welcome in Independence, Missouri. Their daughter was married in 1956 in the same Trinity Episcopal Church in which Harry and Bess where married 37 years before. In 1969 they quietly celebrated their 50th wedding anniversary. Harry died in 1972 at 88 and Bess lived until 1982, dying at 97.

"She was made of equal parts of goodness and granite."
Edith Helm,
Secretary to
Bess Truman

Bess's faith is described as "deep down and personal," consistent with her persona. Although not an active church attendee, Bess was a spiritual person. Her daughter described her mother's faith as a faith close to that of her pioneer ancestors. Her faith centered on a caring, loving God. When Harry tried to get Bess to provide religious instruction for Margaret, Bess enrolled her in a Sunday school. Margaret did not like the Sunday school and convinced her mother that she would learn just as much by going to church with her every time her mother went. Her mother agreed and Margaret claimed it as a victory, since her mother seldom went to church.

This proud, private lady from Independence kept her spirit and confidence for almost thirty years after leaving the White House. Only those closest to her were able to delight in her wit, her comfort, and her astute perceptions. Jackie Kennedy remarked that she admired Bess Truman the most of any of the First Ladies, because she was able to successfully raise a child in the White

House. Bess did that and much more. She provided the love, the support, and the sounding board the president needed during one of the most crucial times in our country's history.

Lessons from Bess

For God has not given us the spirit of fear; but of power, and of love, and of a sound mind (2 Timothy 1:7).

The lessons we learn from Bess are those of perseverance, consistency, and devotion. Bess did not want to be First Lady and fought with clenched lips and stiff back any attempts to make her into the social hostess of the nation. She was her own person and planned to stay that way. She did thaw some after the election in 1948 when Truman won on his own, and Bess actually began accepting her role and enjoying the White House. But for Bess, Harry and Margaret were first and foremost in her life. The fame and power never swayed her from her mission. Being First Lady was simply a necessary chore to be tolerated. The lesson we learn from her is to keep priorities straight, and to refrain from being distracted by the glitter and glamour of an outside world that flutters temptation in front of our faces. Bess knew her place. She was clear about her purposes. And she was never swayed.

Dear God, slow us down. Help us to focus. Help us to keep our priorities straight, to serve You and our families without distraction or resentment or regret or longing for things that are completely unimportant. Amen.

34

ꝏꝏꝏ

Mamie Geneva Doud Eisenhower

"A patient wife in pink and curls"

Meet Mamie

Born	Iowa, 1896
Married	Dwight D. Eisenhower, 1916
Children	Two sons (one died in childhood)
First Lady	1953–1961
Died	1979 at age 82
Mamie's World	Korean War ends; religious revival sweeps across the country; Elvis hits the Top Ten.

For most First Ladies, the White House was a very temporary dwelling, but for Mamie, the White House was the first and most permanent home she had ever known. General Eisenhower was career Army, and they moved 27 times in the 37 years of their marriage. Ike was a military hero in World War II, having served as the Supreme Commander in the war in the Pacific. He retired from the military in 1948 to become president of Columbia University, but the civilian interlude didn't last. He was called back in 1950 to become Supreme Allied Commander in Europe.

Although he had never held political office, never voted, and did not even belong to a political party, Ike was persuaded by supporters to run for president of the United States under one of the most famous slogans in American political campaigning: "I like Ike!" He won the nomination and the presidency in 1952 and again in 1956.

"I can't speak for any other marriage, but the secret of our marriage is that we have absolutely nothing in common."
Mamie Eisenhower

The Eisenhowers had two children: Doud Dwight ("Icky") who died at age five in 1921, and a second son John, born in 1922. (John grew up to be a career military officer like his father, an author, and the ambassador to Belgium.) When John was in combat in the Army, Mamie demonstrated profound faith: All she could do, she said, was "pray without ceasing—just as I prayed for his father. Only with Johnnie, Ike prayed with me—and that helped."

While Ike ran the country, First Lady Mamie ran the White House. She did not get involved in any political matters. She proudly stated that she had been in Ike's office only four times in eight years, and she had been invited each time. She was a strict manager of the White House, but made it a warm and livable

Mamie and Ike at the airport.

space, even if she decorated the family areas in all pink and green. She was a gracious hostess and averaged over 700 visitors a day their first year in the White House.

Suffering from a rheumatic heart and inner ear problems, Mamie needed extra rest and frequently ran the affairs of the East Wing from her bedroom. Whatever her schedule, she always tried to be free for the soap opera "As the World Turns" every afternoon.

After the White House, Mamie and Ike retired to the house they had built in Gettysburg, Pennsylvania. For the first time in their lives, they lived in a home of their own. They lived a quiet, peaceful life until Ike suffered a series of heart attacks in 1968 and died in 1969. Mamie lived another 10 years, missing Ike, but enjoying her home and her four grandchildren.

Mamie grew up in the Presbyterian Church. For her, church was very much a social and family affair. It's important to note that Mamie was an Army wife. She traveled with her husband and was accustomed to military chaplains all over the world. She was probably not particularly affiliated with one denomination to the exclusion of all others. The Army has three denominations: Protestant, Catholic, and Jewish. There are no specific distinctions within any of the three, so Mamie was probably general in the practice of her faith.

There is a story told of Mamie having trouble keeping a straight face with Ike and their friends in a strict chaplain's service in Puerto Rico, so she probably had a lot of fun and was likely a little irreverent

Ike was a religious man and the first president to begin his Inaugural Address with a prayer. He also opened every cabinet meeting with silent prayer. Over the years, President Eisenhower had come forward as a dedicated soldier and statesman who declared his faith in God. Mamie, though she had not been articulate in a public expression, had equal religious conviction, and turned daily to the Bible and books of spiritual comfort and guidance. Only frail health occasionally prevented her from going to church with her husband.

After Ike's fourth heart attack, Mamie stayed in the hospital with him for almost eleven months. Mamie was by his side when his heart finally gave out in March of 1969. During the funeral services, Mamie was praised as the faithful companion who graciously shared her husband with the world. Mamie, who never cried in public, finally wept at the end of the service as the final hymn, *Onward Christian Soldiers*, was sung. Her soldier was going onward.

Lessons From Mamie

I will lift up mine eyes unto the hills, from whence cometh my help (Psalms 121:1).

Yea, I have loved thee with an everlasting love (Jeremiah 31:3).

From Mamie we learn to use the talents God gives us and in all circumstances, be the people we are. Mamie's daughter-in-law remarked that Mamie was exactly as she seemed. There were no pretensions, no hidden self. She took her talents and used them to the benefit of her husband and the country. The other lesson from Mamie is that home isn't a place you live; it's a place in your heart. She followed Ike for nearly all their lives together, and managed to make homes out of a seemingly endless succession of military quarters. While Ike made his career serving his country first as a General and then as president, her job was to make sure that each impersonal space was filled with enough love and familiarity that wherever the Eisenhowers lived was the Eisenhower HOME. Home is where the heart is.

Dear God, help us to be helpmeets. Remind us always that You are our refuge and our hiding place. No matter where we are on earth, we are safe with You until You bring us home. Amen.

35

Jacqueline Lee Bouvier Kennedy

"People have told me 99 things that I had to do as First Lady and I haven't done one of them." Jackie

◈ Meet Jackie

Born	New York, 1929
Married	John F. Kennedy, 1953
	Aristotle Onassis, 1968
Children	Three (one died in infancy)
First Lady	1961-63
Died	1994 at age 64
Jackie's World	Peace Corps established; Civil Rights demonstrations rage; Alan Shepard is America's first man in space.

Jackie! Just the name inspired and fascinated millions. Jack and Jackie were the United States' own prince and princess. They were young, beautiful, sophisticated, and wealthy. Jack won every election he ever entered, and he entered the White House in 1961 as our youngest president ever. The Kennedy administration, with all its glamour and splendor, was called "Camelot."

Jackie was born to wealthy parents and educated in private schools. She was mentioned in the society pages even as a child. She loved dogs and horses, and was an accomplished equestrian. She attended Vassar, the Sorbonne, and George Washington University before landing a job at the Washington Times-Herald. She met Jack in 1951, and by 1953 they were married.

Jackie's passion was for the arts, but Jack's was for politics. It was a passion shared by his entire family. She was amazed and sometimes troubled by the competitiveness of the Kennedys and their zeal for getting Jack into the White House.

Everything about the First Lady (she hated the term) was fuel for the media. She worked to protect the privacy of her children, but they were the darlings of the press. Even though she shielded her home from the press, she didn't shield the White House. In fact, she put it front stage center. Her favorite project was the restoration of the White House, and she personally hosted an

Jack, Jackie, Caroline, and John-John.

Jackie gives a tour of the White House on national television.

hour-long television tour of the mansion in 1962 when history lessons and interior design merged to give the American public a sense of pride.

All was not rosy in the private quarters of the White House. Jack was concerned about her extravagant spending, and she learned of his philandering. Slipping quietly from constant media attention and scrutiny, Jackie limited her social schedule in order to have playtime with her children, Caroline and "John-John," every day, and frequently escaped the White House for periods of seclusion and privacy.

"If you bungle raising your children, I don't think whatever else you do matters very much."
Jackie Kennedy

Camelot came to a brutal end in 1963 with the assassination of Jack in a motorcade in Dallas, Texas. The nation and the world went into mourning, but the composure and serenity of Jackie inspired and comforted all who saw her.

Her popularity didn't end with her departure from the White House. She was pursued and photographed all of her life. Her marriage to Aristotle Onassis in 1968, a billionaire almost 30 years her senior, shocked and outraged many, but did nothing to lessen the public's obsession with her. After his death,

Jackie's painting of an angel was sold as boxed Christmas cards to raise funds for a National Cultural Center in Washington, DC.

she returned to New York City, where she could "blend in" with other high profile people, work as a book editor, and lead life quietly.

Of her faith we know very little. She was Catholic, but did not appear to seek solace in the church. Despite her beauty, wit, and wealth, life for Jackie was a series of tragedies. Virtually every man in her life died an untimely death, first her father, then her infant son, then her husband when she was only 34, then her favorite brother-in-law, Robert Kennedy, and her second husband Ari when she was still only 46. The senselessness of the assassinations of Jack and Robert caused her to proclaim bitterly, "The Catholic Church understands death. I'll tell you who else understands death are the black churches. I remember at the funeral of Martin Luther King, Jr., I was looking at those faces, and I realized that they knew death. They see it all the time and they are ready for it... in a way in which a good Catholic is. We know death. As a matter of fact, if it weren't for the children, we'd welcome it."

Jackie was spared another tragedy, the early death of her only son, John, by dying of cancer in 1994.

Jackie was the most photographed and studied First Lady of all time, yet we know little about the real woman. She played her public role with aplomb, but she cherished and shielded her private self. Her most enduring legacy is that of a forgiving wife and a ferociously devoted mother. Both of her children grew up as normally as she could manage, and both became highly successful, talented, charming, dignified people. She must have been proud. She had every right to be.

Lessons from Jackie

Blessed are they that mourn: for they shall be comforted (Matthew 5:4).

For wisdom is better than rubies; and all the things that are to be desired are not to be compared to it (Proverbs 9:11).

Happiness cannot be found in wealth, power, beauty, or fame. Jackie had all of these and still found the world wanting. She was betrayed by her husband. And even though she was a worthy wife and helpmate, she never found acceptance from his family. She had millions of fans, but only a few real friends. And the joy in her life was marred by the deaths of people she loved. Yet it can be said of Jackie that she handled it all with great dignity and grace, and seemed to prevail over sorrow to create a good life for herself and her children.

The second lesson from Jackie is that of devoting oneself to the rearing of children, precious gifts from God given to one's keeping. No matter what else was going on in her life, Jackie put her children first, protecting them and giving them the best that she had to give, all the time, and putting no on above them.

Dear God, thank You for the gifts of family and children. Help us to be worthy. Give us the wisdom to rear them in Your ways, to help them grow and flourish in the abundance, love and glory of Your kingdom. Amen.

36

Claudia (Lady Bird) Alta Taylor Johnson

When you see wildflowers along the highway,
enjoy the moment and thank Lady Bird.

Meet Lady Bird

Born	Texas, 1912
Married	Lyndon B. Johnson, 1934
Children	Two daughters
First Lady	1963-1969
Lady Bird's World	Civil Rights Act passes; Vietnam War escalates; Martin Luther King assassinated; waterbeds and Woodstock debut.

Lady Bird was 50 when she was thrust into the White House. She was a veteran on the Washington scene, accustomed to campaigning and entertaining after more than twenty-five years in the political arena. But even still, she felt ill equipped and apprehensive about her new role. She once quipped that if she'd known she was going to be First Lady, she would have fixed two things: her name and her nose.

Many people's earliest memory of Lady Bird Johnson is the stoic, shocked image of her standing beside her husband in Air Force One as Johnson was sworn in as 36th president of the United States the same day Kennedy was assassinated in Dallas. For the seventh time, the vice president was called suddenly to lead the nation through mourning and rebuilding.

Lady Bird's mother died when she was six and her Aunt Effie reared her. She attended a one-room schoolhouse on the family ranch until she was 13, when she drove herself to the local high school 14 miles away. She attended an Episcopal school for a short while and then graduated from the University of Texas at Austin in the top 10 percent of her class. While in Austin she met the young Lyndon, who proposed to her the day after they met. She said no. Undaunted and persistent, Lyndon proposed again the same week. She managed to hold him off a whole two months before they were married in San Antonio. She was still debating whether or not to go through with the ceremony as they walked into the church. The best man had to run to a Sears store across the street to buy a $2.50 wedding ring. Even the minister had doubts that the marriage would last, but last it did.

"I feel I am suddenly on stage for a part I never rehearsed."
Lady Bird Johnson

Early in their marriage, Lady Bird took money from her inheritance and bought a nearly bankrupt small radio station. Within a year she made a very small profit, but in the next 20 years, she managed to turn it into a multi-million dollar broadcasting company. Starting a family proved more difficult, but after 10 years and four miscarriages they had a daughter and three years later a second daughter.

Lady Bird was a good nickname for the First Lady who was as close to nature and the causes of environmental protection as few First Ladies had been. She declared "Beautification" as her cause and worked for years to promote highway programs, gardens, parks, and forests. Her Highway Beautification project—the planting of wildflowers along major highways—limited billboards and certainly made the roadways look more festive. But more than pretty posies were at stake. Lady Bird's simple flowers shut down some strip-mining operations and stopped environmental destruction, because the mines were not allowed to disturb the wildflower plantings. She also worked promoting her husband's "War on Poverty," visiting depressed areas in Appalachia and rural and urban schools.

When Lyndon declined to run for a second term, they retired to their Texas ranch. Lady Bird continued to manage her businesses and remained active in beautification projects.

Of Lady Bird's faith, we know that when she was a student at St. Mary's Episcopal School for Girls in Dallas, she was required to attend daily chapel and Sunday services. Although only fifteen, this experience provided a religious framework that she maintained throughout her life. She regularly attended church and remained devoted to her husband and marriage despite dalliances on Lyndon's part. After retirement, she started each day with a devotional reading and ended each night with her Bible.

Lady Bird is consistently ranked as one of our most impressive and active First Ladies. She did it all—from campaigning, to causes, to protecting the president and holding the family together. It was pure love that drove her.

Lessons from Lady Bird

Behold, I will do a new thing: now it shall spring forth; shall ye not know it? I will even make a way in the wilderness, and rivers in the desert (Isaiah 43:19).

Let the sea roar, and the fullness thereof: let the fields rejoice and all that is therein. Then shall the trees of the wood sing out at the presence of the Lord (1 Chronicles 16:32-33).

From Lady Bird we learn to take time to see the beauty of the earth, and glory in the marvels of nature. Lady Bird realized that the environment was not indestructible and that if we wanted our grandchildren to see a mountain, or a canyon, or even wildflowers we had to invest in our world. She recognized God's world for the wonder that it is. But she also recognized our role as stewards of the gifts. Very simply, we have to take care of the earth. And if we do our jobs well, perhaps the earth will be better for its having been momentarily in our care.

Dear God, let us not gaze at a mountain, a river, a tree, or a blossom without seeing Your hand. Thank You for the bounty and the beauty. May we be good stewards of Your work and good servants in Your service. Amen.

37

Thelma (Pat) Catherine Ryan Nixon

*"She had given so much to the nation and to the world.
Her only reward was to share my exile. She deserved so
much more." Richard Nixon*

Meet Pat

Born	Nevada, 1912
Married	Richard M. Nixon, 1940
Children	Two daughters
First Lady	1969-1974
Died	1993 at age 81
Pat's World	Neil Armstrong takes the first moon walk; the National Guard fires on war protesters in the infamous Kent State shootings; *Godspell* and *Jesus Christ Superstar* are Broadway hits.

From the pinnacle of power and prestige to the depths of disgrace and disaster, Pat held on with white knuckles and a tight smile. Most people have to contend with peaks and valleys in their lives, but few experience the extreme highs and lows that chronicled Pat Nixon's life. Thelma Catherine was nicknamed "Pat" by her father because she was born on St. Patrick's Day eve. But for Pat, the luck of the Irish eluded her.

Pat's family moved to California when she was two. Her father tried to support the family with a small truck farm. The whole family worked in the fields. Her mother died when she was 13, and Pat took over the housework and the cooking in addition to going to school and working in the fields. Her father became ill when she was 15, and she cared for him until he died two years later. She finished high school and worked in a bank, a hospital and as a secretary for two years before enrolling in the University of Southern California. She worked her way through college grading papers, store clerking and as a movie extra. In 1937, she landed her first professional job as a schoolteacher in the Quaker community of Whittier, California. When she tried out for the community theater, she met the young attorney in town, Richard Nixon. He proposed at the first rehearsal, which wasn't in the script. She made him wait two years. They were married in a Quaker ceremony when she was 28 and he 27. She continued teaching until they moved to Washington and he joined the Navy.

To say that Pat disliked politics is an understatement. She thought politicians were the most vicious people on earth. But Richard loved the power and limelight and thrived on the campaigns. He was elected to Congress in 1947 and as vice president under Eisenhower in 1952. After each election, Richard pledged to Pat not to run again, but he never kept his promises. After eight years as vice president, which included a scandal concerning their finances, Nixon ran for president and lost to Kennedy in 1960. Then he ran for governor of California in 1962 and lost again.

Pat and daughter Julie are beseiged by the media while Christmas shopping.

He pledged again in writing, if not in blood, never to run for public office. But 1968 saw Nixon running for president and winning. Pat felt betrayed, but adjusted as always and worked hard at managing the White House and her family. She did not get involved in any political matters, but did become a goodwill ambassador and traveled around the world. She tried to promote "volunteerism' as a cause and successfully continued the restoration of the White House begun by Jackie Kennedy. She also was responsible for the outside lighting of the White House.

There were two Pats: the political, public Pat—the role she hated (and it showed), and the real Pat—mother, wife, homemaker, and diplomat. Although labeled as "plastic" and a "robot," Pat was actually a compassionate, warm person who improved international relations with goodwill mission trips to Vietnam, Peru, and Liberia.

Despite successes in space exploration and foreign policy, the Watergate affair tainted all of the Nixon administration. A burglary of the Democratic National Headquarters located in the Watergate office complex in Washington, D.C. catapulted into the biggest scandal of the decade. White House aides and advisors were convicted of conspiracy and implicated the president. Nixon initially refused to release tape recordings from his office, claiming executive privilege. This and other charges prompted Congress to start impeachment hearings against Nixon for obstruction of justice and abuses of power. Fearing impeachment, Nixon resigned in 1974. He was the first president to resign from office. It was a devastating blow to him and his entire family.

Pat maintained a stoic reserve throughout the Watergate affair. She had advised her husband to destroy his private tapes months before the investigation started, but he rarely involved her in any of his affairs and did not take her well-intentioned advice. She continued to stand close by him throughout the ordeal, just as she had all of their married life.

Their life improved after the White House. They moved back to California and eventually to New Jersey to be near their grandchildren. Pat suffered a stroke in 1976, but recovered and enjoyed her retirement and gardening until she died in 1993.

Pat was a Congregationalist, but adopted many of the Quaker beliefs of her husband. She initiated a Sunday prayer service in the East Room that drew several hundred attendees every week. It was a deeply religious service and meaningful not only in its substance, but also in the partakers. It was open to every level of government worker, with secretaries and aides and senators all bowing in prayer together.

Lessons from Pat

Humble yourselves therefore under the almighty hand of God, that he may exalt you in due time (1 Peter 5:6).

Behold, I send you forth as sheep in the midst of wolves: be ye therefore as wise as serpents and harmless as doves (Matthew 10:16).

The disciple is not above his master, nor the servant above his lord (Matthew 10:24).

Pat Nixon taught us that even in our deepest despair, there is always hope. She had a hard life, but she never gave up. Even when her husband refused to listen to her or take into consideration any of her needs, she stood by his side, chin up, eyes straight ahead. She must have repeated the old Quaker belief, "There is that of God in every man." hundreds of times as she struggled with the challenges of having to leave the White House under suspicion of crimes committed by her husband. She said, "I love my husband. I believe in him, and I am proud of his accomplishments." Loyalty is the second lesson of Pat Nixon. We'll never know what she thought privately, or what conversations transpired between Richard and her, but we do know that in public, she never wavered her unyielding support. Her love was there for all to see.

Dear God, let us see the good in people. Teach us to forgive those who trespass against us, and to love them with the love of Christ. Amen.

38

Elizabeth (Betty) Bloomer Warren Ford

"It doesn't matter by whose hand a life is saved. It's always the hand of God anyway." Betty Ford

Meet Betty

Born	Illinois, 1918
Married	William Warren, 1942
	Gerald Ford, 1948
Children	Four (three sons and one daughter)
First Lady	1974-1977
Betty's World	The Vietnam War ends; America celebrates its Bicentennial; the Sears Tower in Chicago becomes the world's tallest building; the movie *Star Wars* debuts.

Betty loved to dance. She grew up in Michigan and starting dancing when she was eight, graduating from the Calla Travis Dance Studio and then studying under Martha Graham at the Bennington School of Dance in Vermont. She worked as a professional dancer and model for two years in New York City. She married a salesman in 1942, but they divorced five years later, and Betty married Jerry Ford, graduate of Yale and football hero, just three weeks before he was elected to Congress.

Being the wife of a congressman turned out to be more painful, stressful, and debilitating than being a dancer. She suffered continual pain from a pinched nerve and sought psychiatric counseling. In 1973, after 25 years in Congress, Betty had convinced Jerry to retire from politics. But instead of retirement, Nixon appointed Jerry as his vice president after the resignation of Spiro Agnew. Just a year later, the Watergate scandal exploded, Nixon himself resigned, and the Fords suddenly found themselves in the White House. This was not what Betty had in mind when she suggested that it was time to retire.

Betty might have been a dancer, but she never danced around the issues. She was willing to talk about anything and her honest, direct replies might have caused ulcers with her husband's

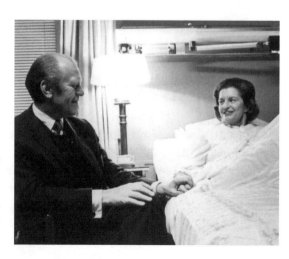

In 1974, Betty Ford announced to the nation that she had breast cancer. Here President Ford is shown visiting her in the hospital.

politicos, but they won her the admiration of the public. Instead of a muzzle, Jerry gave her a megaphone. She spoke publicly about her dependency on painkillers and alcohol, her battle with breast cancer, and her psychiatric counseling. Her courage to speak up— honestly, personally, and candidly— saved other woman's lives when she gave them the courage to seek treatment for their own illnesses. She also worked for ratification of the Equal Rights Amendment and the appointment of more women in government positions. Instead of being a liability to her husband's career, she was a great asset. Reelection buttons proclaimed "Betty's Husband for President!"

I. Betty Ford campaign button

Gerald Ford did not win reelection and he and Betty retired to California where Betty continued her work for women's rights, cancer research and rehabilitation. Her own personal problems did not decrease and she had to enter a residential program for alcohol and drug dependency. She in turn worked to establish the Betty Ford Center for Drug and Alcohol Rehabilitation, a world famous facility credited with saving thousands of lives.

In Betty's autobiography, *A Glad Awakening*, she describes the profound effect God has had on her recovery and life after the White House. She found joy only after she stopped trying to direct God, but let God do the work. Her autobiography is a beacon for sufferers and families looking for support and encouragement. She speaks with candor and knowledge. "God has allowed me—along with thousands of others—to carry a message, a message that says, there's help out there, and you too can be a survivor." Yes, she is a survivor, but also a hero for opening doors and shining light on women's issues and concerns that had been kept in the shadows for centuries.

Lessons from Betty

Confess your faults one to another, and pray one for another, that ye may be healed. The effectual fervent prayer of a righteous man availeth much (James 5:16).

Betty is a lesson in courage. How far we have come from the age of Martha Washington and Abigail Adams when a proper lady's name was never found in print and a lady never spoke or wrote anything for the public. Even obituaries for women 200 years ago only listed the deceased as "wife of..." instead of her given name. Betty's fore-sisters certainly paved the way, but Betty took giant steps and was not afraid to open her frailties and faults to the world. The response was not consternation or contempt, but acceptance and ovation. Openness and honesty: what a unique political ploy! More politicians should try it. We also learned, thanks to Betty, that all people have problems, and we can take heart that even the top family in the country is not immune to pain and addictions. Thanks to Betty, thousands more have taken those same brave steps and prayed the prayer of their salvation.

The Serenity Prayer

God grant me the Serenity
To accept the things I cannot change;
Courage to change the things that I can;
and Wisdom to know the difference.

Living one day at a time;
Enjoying one moment at a time;
Accepting hardship
as the pathway to peace;

Taking, as He did,
this sinful world as it is,
not as I would have it;

Trusting that He will make
all things right if I
surrender to His will;

That I may be reasonably
happy in this life, and
supremely happy with Him
forever in the next.
Amen.

By Reinhold Niebuhr,
Protestant theologian

39
❧

Rosalynn Smith Carter

*"I had already learned from more than a decade of political life
that I was going to be criticized no matter what I did, so I might
as well be criticized for something I wanted to do."* *Rosalynn Carter*

▨ *Meet Rosalynn*

Born	Georgia, 1927
Married	Jimmy Carter, 1946
Children	Four (three sons, 1 daughter)
First Lady	1977–1981
Rosalynn's World	The United States boycotts the Olympic Games to protest Soviet invasion of Afghanistan; Iran holds 52 Americans hostage for over a year; disco dancing and the Trivial Pursuit game are hot fads.

A high school valedictorian, Rosalynn was the pride of Plains, Georgia. Her father had died when she was 13, and Rosalynn worked hard to please and support her mother, attending a nearby junior college in order to remain near home. Another pride of Plains was just graduating from the United States Naval Academy, and when smitten Rosalynn saw young Jimmy Carter in his white uniform, it was the start of a lifelong partnership. She was only 18 when they were married, but she was ready to get out of Plains and the Navy gave her the way out. Seven years later, Jimmy's father died and Jimmy decided to resign from the Navy and return to Plains to run the family peanut business. Rosalynn did not want to return to Georgia and they argued for days, but she lost that round.

The peanut business thrived under her watchful eye, only to be traded for a life in politics and a walk into the White House, where her personal staff alone was twice the number of her high school class.

Visitors on the morning tour watch as Rosalynn Carter greets young guests in the Blue Room. The First Lady would often drop in on tours unannounced to welcome surprised sightseers to their national home.

Rosalynn, Amy, and Jimmie Carter in front of the White House Christmas tree in 1977.

The road to the White House was paved with public offices. Jimmy became a state senator and then governor of Georgia. Rosalynn overcame her fear of public speaking and soon became a strong campaigner. When Jimmy was elected president, she continued her active involvement, conferring daily with him on a wide range of relevant issues. She attended cabinet meetings, visited foreign leaders as representative of the president, and appeared before congressional subcommittees. Our most active First Lady since Eleanor Roosevelt, Rosalynn gave hundreds of speeches and interviews. Although criticized by some as having too much power, Rosalynn was simply serving as her husband's most trusted and loyal advisor, a role she took seriously and performed as well as, if not better than any highly paid appointee.

Mental Health issues became her cause celebré, and she worked to get health insurance coverage, community facilities, and services for those with mental illnesses. Her causes expanded to include the Equal Rights Amendment, refugee assistance and care for the elderly. Rosalynn did not focus on Washington's social scene or on any renovation projects.

After leaving the White House, the Carters' political, community, and international involvement did not end, but increased. They became active supporters of Habitat for Humanity, helping to build houses for the poor all over the world. They remained active in their local church where the Jimmy Carter Sunday School Class is probably the biggest Sunday School class in Georgia, if not the country.

Rosalynn's early life in Plains revolved around the churches. Her grandmother was Lutheran, her grandfather Baptist, and her parents Methodist, so she was *always* at church. But religion was more than just church attendance for Rosalynn. God was always a part of her life. Her mother read to her from the Bible every night. Her parents also respected and admired the Carters, especially Jimmy's mother, Lillian Carter, a registered nurse who willingly and graciously treated everyone in the county regardless of race or status. Rosalynn's sister was named Lillian in honor of Jimmy's mother. When Rosalynn and Jimmy returned to Plains after the Navy, she joined the Baptist Church. They were one of the few families in town to stand up for integration of the churches. An active and influential woman throughout her life, Rosalynn never forgot or abandoned her strong religious and humanitarian roots.

Lessons from Rosalynn

Two are better than one; because they have a good reward for their labour. For if they fall, the one will lift up his fellow: but woe to him that is alone when he falleth; for he hath not another to help him up (Ecclesiastics 4: 9-10).

From Rosalynn we learn that we can go home again. With the understanding that we are not the same people as when we left, and that home may also not be the same place we remember. Time does not stand still, even in Plains, Georgia. After the Navy, Rosalynn hated the idea of returning to Plains. She saw it only as a step backwards ... and Rosalynn always wanted to plow ahead. But the return was vital for the rest of their successes (the operative word being "their"). If ever there was a working partnership, it was Rosalynn and Jimmy. From the peanut farm to the Governor's mansion and the White House, the public got two for one.

Although the Carters were dedicated and hard working, they didn't have a network in Washington. They were the outsiders, too prim and busy for the social set, and too new and unseasoned for the political set. It was only after the White House, when they returned to Plains one more time, that they truly succeeded. Jimmy is still called upon as a skilled diplomat and Rosalynn has never slowed down with her church and charities. The Carters are still making a difference from Plains for the whole world.

Dear God, **remind us that we need to grow where we're planted, and that our life circumstances are a function of Your plan. Keep us mindful that the power to change the world doesn't come from capitals, courts, and palaces. It comes through You, working through us. Amen.**

40

Anne Frances (Nancy) Davis Reagan

"Neither marriage nor politics denies a spouse the right to hold an opinion or the right to express it." Nancy Reagan

Meet Nancy

Born	New York, 1921
Married	Ronald Reagan, 1952
Children	Two
First Lady	1981-1989
Nancy's World	Iran-Contra Affair erupts; Challenger Space Shuttle explodes; first artificial heart is implanted; "New Coke" flubs; old Coke reintroduced as "Coke Classic."

After two years in the White House, former Hollywood actress Nancy Reagan had nowhere to go but up. She had been ridiculed, lampooned, and roasted in every newspaper, gossip column, and late night talk show for lavish spending and entertaining. She saw her response to criticism as "serene." The public saw her as "aloof." Political party advisors decided that she was a liability, and if Ronald Reagan were to win reelection, the First Lady had to be remade into a kinder, gentler, more responsible Nancy. With a dedication to her husband that bordered on obsession, Nancy Reagan did an about-face with humor and perseverance. No one would ever accuse Nancy of being a political liability again; she was forevermore the quintessential "wife." Once, responding to complaints that she wielded too much power in the White House, she quipped, "This morning I had planned to clear up US-Soviet differences on intermediate-range nuclear missiles. But I decided to clean out Ronnie's sock drawer instead."

From poverty to power is a recurring theme in the First Ladies' histories, and Anne (Nancy) Frances Robbins Davis Reagan is no exception. Nancy's father abandoned her mother shortly after she was born. Her mother was an actress and left Nancy with an aunt to be raised. Her life began an upward spiral when her mother remarried, this time to a wealthy physician who adopted her and

Nancy looks at Ronnie with the famous "gaze."

Nancy Reagan introduced a lighter American cuisine into the White House menu.

sent her to private schools and college. Nancy majored in drama at Smith College and became an actress in New York and Hollywood. In 1949 she moved to Hollywood and met Ronald Reagan. They married in 1952 and she gave up her movie career to be a full-time wife and mother.

Ronald retired from the screen and entered politics as governor of California in 1966 and president in 1980. As noted earlier, Nancy's first two years as First Lady in the White House weren't easy; she was highly criticized. With advisors' help, she worked hard to change her image, and adopted drug awareness as her cause. Her "Just Say No" campaigns were well received, and she traveled all over the country to educate children on the dangers of illegal drugs. Being seen on the evening news, smiling with school children, did a lot to improve her image. The country warmed up.

When historians look back on the Reagan administration, they'll surely note a number of accomplishments, but the signature of the Reagans will likely be their love for each other. Nancy frequently claimed that her first priority was her husband. She stayed close by his side, particularly after the failed assassination attempt on his life. In fact, she was so protective that she would abide no criticism of the president, and worked to remove any staff that she thought were problematic.

If anyone thought that the starry-eyed romance of the Reagans was a good front put on by two former Hollywood actors for the benefit of the public, all doubts have been erased. In the solitude and secrecy of private life, Nancy Reagan demonstrated steadfast devotion by caring for and protecting an increasingly debilitated Ronald Reagan, who developed Alzheimer's disease, announced in 1993. Living in California, she made very few public appearances and allowed none for her beloved Ronnie. She made sure that he is remembered as the dignified, capable, handsome leader and leading man that she married. Ronald Reagan passed away June 5, 2004.

"A woman is like a teabag—only in hot water do you realize how strong she is."
Nancy Reagan

Little is known of Nancy's faith. Neither her autobiographical works nor her daughter's book make even a mention. But we do know that Ronald Reagan was a member of the Disciples of Christ Church and was a deeply religious man of God. The Reagans were married in the Little Brown Church, and the name of their first ranch was God's Little Eight Acres, so we do know that she lived in a godly home with a godly man. We can only assume that she, herself, is a woman of faith, but perhaps the details of it are kept as secret as so many things in her life. One Nancy-watcher wryly said, "She believes in astrology and Ronald Reagan." But we know there's more.

Lessons from Nancy

Turn away mine eyes from beholding vanity and quicken thou me in thy way (Psalm 119:37).

Nancy went from the glitter of Hollywood to the White House and forgot to change her shoes. Lavish clothes and entertainment labeled her as an actress playing her biggest role instead of a sincere, committed First Lady. But she did listen to advisors who helped her find a new direction, and was capable of making change. We all can change, no matter what path we are on or how long we have been on the wrong road. We have a light, a guidebook, and a Savior.

The other lesson from Nancy is that a helpmate's job is not only to help, but also to protect. No matter how much criticism came her way, Nancy Reagan was fully capable of stepping from behind her husband to throw herself between him and anyone who would do him harm. There's steel in that kind of devotion.

Dear God, **lift away our old clothes, our sins, and our vanities, and teach us humility. When we have erred, please forgive us and give us the wisdom, character, and humilty to make right all that we've done wrong and keep from repeating our mistakes. Help us to love with the same sacrificial love of Christ. Amen.**

41
❧

Barbara Pierce Bush

*"You really only have two choices. You can like what you do,
or you can dislike it. I choose to like it, and what fun I've had."*
Barbara Bush

Meet Barbara

Born	New York, 1925
Married	George Bush, 1945
Children	Six (one died in childhood)
First Lady	1989-1993
Barbara's World	The Berlin Wall falls; the United States leads forces into Iraq in the Persian Gulf War; Johnny Carson retires from the *Tonight Show*.

At Bush family reunions, the Secret Service men probably outnumber the grandchildren. But that is to be expected in a family with a former president, a current president, and a governor all sitting around the same table. The head of this famous crew? None other than everybody's grandmother, Barbara Bush. Not since Abigail Adams has a woman been the wife of one president and the mother of another.

Barbara was born into a wealthy New York family and educated in private schools in New York and South Carolina. She first met George (Poppy) Bush in 1941 at a Christmas Party but George returned to high school in Connecticut and then entered the Navy and Barbara finished high school and entered Smith College. Her heart wasn't in school, it was somewhere in the South Pacific. She did meet George's parents in 1943, and the grand matriarch, Dorothy Bush, gave her approval of Barbara, mainly because she was spontaneous and could play a fair game of tennis. She and George became engaged that year and married in 1945. They moved to Texas where George started and succeeded in the oil business until entering politics in 1966. He served in the House

Despite her image as a white-haired grandmother, Barbara Bush maintained a physically active lifestyle. Here she is seen biking with "First Dog" Millie.

Barbara Bush kept a diary on her own personal computer. She was the first First Lady to use this technology.

of Representatives, the United Nations, the CIA, and as vice-president under Ronald Reagan. Barbara agreed to help campaign in 1988, only if she didn't have to dye her hair, change her dress, or lose any weight. When George won the presidential election in 1988, Barbara was sixty-three and everybody loved her just as she was.

She was an active First Lady and promoted literacy as her special project. In fact, she edited a best-selling children's book while in the White House: *Millie's Book*, an autobiography by their extremely literate First Dog, Millie. The entire proceeds of which went to the Barbara Bush Foundation for Family Literacy. She was also active in projects for the homeless, and was honorary chair of the Leukemia Society.

Tragedy struck the Bush family early when their daughter, Robin, died of leukemia when she was only 3 years old. Barbara described in her book, *Memoirs* that she never felt God as close as when Robin slipped away. Barbara knew that her child's soul was with God.

"Your success as a family, our success as a society, depends not on what happens in the White House, but on what happens inside your house."
Barbara Bush

For Barbara, religion was close and personal. In "Memoirs" she shares a letter that she wrote her children in 1993 but never sent: "I would certainly say, above all, seek God. He will come to you if you look. There is absolutely NO down side. Please expose your children and set a good example for them by going to church. We, your Dad and I, have tried to live as Christian a life as we can. We certainly have not been perfect. Maybe you can! Keep trying." What wonderful advice from the White House or any house.

Lessons from Barbara

As one whom his mother comforteth, so will I comfort you (Isaiah 66:13).

Train up a child in the way he should go: and when he is old, he will not depart from it (Proverbs 22:6).

Barbara's first lesson is to acknowledge that motherhood is the hardest, most terrifying, most rewarding job on earth. How do you know when to control and when to let go, when to comfort and when to confront? Kids don't come with instructions! Motherhood starts and ends with unconditional love. The template for this patient, compassionate, sacrificial, tender love is the love that God has for us. It pays off. Sometimes it seems to take forever for a child to grow up, but if our love is constant, our wayward, partying kid might just grow up to be president.

Barbara's second lesson is that of accepting and believing in yourself. Her refusal to lose weight or dye her hair for the benefit of public image is a testimony to her strength and self-assurance. In this age of plastic surgery and cosmetic procedures designed to hang onto fleeting youth and superficial beauty, there's something wonderful about a woman who is comfortable in her own skin and who accepts aging with grace and humor as part of God's grand design for her life. Barbara Bush IS beautiful.

Dear God, guide us to be models for our children and our children's children. That they will love us because we first loved them, and that they will know God, because God lived in our home. And teach us to turn our backs on vanity, to be glad in the gifts You have given us. Amen.

43

Hillary Victoria Rodham Clinton

*" I want to live in a country where the care of children
is not determined on whether or not their parents have
health insurance." Hillary Clinton*

Meet Hillary

Born	Illinois, 1947
Married	William Clinton, 1975
Children	One daughter
First Lady	1993-2001
Hillary's World	Personal computers and the internet connect millions; worldwide celebrations for Y2K; *60 Minutes* is the most popular TV show; *Forrest Gump* and *The Lion King* are popular movies.

It would be hard to find two more intelligent, idealistic, public-spirited people than Hillary Rodham and Bill Clinton upon graduation from Yale Law School in 1973. The ink was not yet dry on their respective law degrees when they faced their first dilemma. Bill was committed to returning home and saving Arkansas, and Hillary was committed to staying in the north and saving the world.

After a back and forth relationship, Hillary "followed her heart" to Arkansas and rejoined Bill. Hillary claims that she fell in love with Bill because he was the first guy who wasn't afraid of her. Although many of the previous First Ladies have been better educated and more cultured than their presidential husbands, Hillary is the first whose professional resume and list of accomplishments rival her husband's. They married in 1975. In 1978, President Jimmy Carter appointed Hillary to the board of the Legal Services Corporation, and Bill was elected governor of Arkansas. Governor Clinton served three terms before election as president in 1992. Hillary, First Lady to the governor of Arkansas and mother to daughter Chelsea, continued her own successful career as an attorney in Little Rock and served on many charitable and community boards and action groups. Stamina, discipline and

In July of 1999, Hillary Clinton visited the Saxton-McKinley House to announce aid for the First Ladies' Library from the "Save America's Treasures" program.

intelligence were qualities in a finely honed combination that would well serve Hillary later in the White House.

Hillary grew up in the upper middle class suburb of Park Ridge, near Chicago. She was always a serious student and had a solid public school education in a stable, supportive family. Good schools and a good family gave her the foundation, but the hard work and drive were all Hillary's. She was very competitive and excelled at everything from grade school through law school. She earned every Girl Scout badge, played field hockey and graduated near the top of every school she attended. She loved to debate on any issue, and politics was a hot topic in the radical 60s. Her parents were Republican, so she was a teenaged Goldwater supporter. Four years in the liberal environment of Wellesley College changed her political leanings to Democrat, but also reinforced her deep commitment to public service.

The official White House notes on Hillary list professional and charitable accomplishments, including writing a book about children and winning a Grammy for her recording of it. But truthfully, the tenure of First Lady Hillary Clinton will forever be remembered for scandal and the great dignity with which she handled it.

Hillary served as First Lady during an era in American culture where nearly everyone had access to television and print media, so news traveled fast. But Hillary also had to contend with the Internet, where information was immediate and interactive, international discussions plentiful. To date, if ever a First Lady lived and worked in full public view, it was Hillary. The relentlessness of scrutiny started during Clinton's presidential campaign when he had to explain a former extramarital affair. Hillary stood, smiling and serene, at his side. Probably everyone thought that his repentant manner and her steadfast devotion were sufficient evidence that it was prudent to let bygones be bygones and focus on his abilities as a leader. But Clinton's indiscretions arose again when he had an affair with a White House intern. He was nearly impeached, but acquitted by a narrow margin. The night after his testimony, the Clinton family left Washington to travel to Martha's Vineyard for privacy and rest. Cameras captured their telling and poignant departure: Bill and Hillary walking to the waiting helicopter with daughter Chelsea between them, holding their hands. Ahead of the three, a bounding dog led the way. Hillary wore dark glasses. Later Hillary admitted, "Buddy, the dog, came along to keep Bill company. He was the only member of our family who was still willing to."

Clinton exited the White House under a very black cloud, but Hillary, level and dignified, fared well in the public's perception. She became the first First Lady to enter politics herself and successfully won a seat in the Senate for the state of New York in 2000.

Hillary's faith was sorely tested, but it is a strong, well developed faith, nurtured since childhood. Hillary was christened and confirmed in the Methodist Church, and was a deeply religious person even in high school. She studied Scripture and Christian literature in college. She always carries a small Bible with her. She described her allegiance to the Methodist church as being strong because of its emphasis on personal salvation and social service. "As a Christian, part of my obligation is to take action to alleviate suffering. Explicit recognition of that in the Methodist tradition is one reason I'm comfortable in this church." Scripture and prayer still guide Hillary. She is a strong, pragmatic, driven woman who sincerely believes in making a positive difference in the world.

Lessons from Hillary

***For if ye forgive men their trespasses, your heavenly Father will also forgive you
(Matthew 6:14)***

In an address to the National Prayer Luncheon, Hillary said, "I know in the Bible it says they asked Jesus how many times you should forgive, and He said seventy times seven. Well, I want you to know that I'm keeping a chart." Good humor aside, there was a lot for this wife to forgive, and she seems to have done it.

It was interesting to watch public opinion convict her of being guilty by association ... or at least guilty of having too little character to leave philandering Bill Clinton. But there's also been a groundswell of admiration: men and women who acknowledge that in this "throw-away society" in which we live, where more than half of all marriages end in divorce, there's something strong and wonderful about a woman who loves a man enough to forgive him and who loves her family enough to stay the course, even when it's hard. This is the great lesson of Hillary Clinton: Forgive and forget. The first is very hard, the second almost impossible. But as Christians that is exactly what we are commanded to do. Hurt, anger, and deceit are malignant killers if we allow them to reside in our hearts. We must move on. We are not the judges in this life. Judgment is a terrible burden, and we need to rejoice that it is not ours to bear. All we have to do is forgive.

Hillary frequently quotes John Wesley, founder of Methodism, as her guiding light. "Do all the good you can, by all the means you can, in all the places you can, and all the time you can, to all the people you can, as long as ever you can."

Dear God, please give us the grace and strength to forgive. It's so difficult, but we know that You ask us to forgive so that we can free those who have wronged us, and in doing so, also free ourselves. Forgive us our trespasses as we forgive those who trespass against us. Amen.

43

Laura Lane Welch Bush

*"When we got married my husband promised me that
I would never have to make a speech. So much for
political promises." Laura Bush*

Meet Laura

Born	Texas, 1946
Married	George W. Bush, 1977
Children	Two daughters
First Lady	2001-
Laura's World	September 11, 2001, terrorists highjack commercial jets, flying two into the Twin Towers of the World Trade Center in New York City, flying one into the Pentagon in Washington, DC, and crashing one in a field in Pennsylvania; the United States declares war on Iraq.

George W. Bush, young jet pilot moved into the "wild side" of the apartment complex in Houston, and partied hard whenever he wasn't flying. This congressman's son seemed to meet every single woman in the complex except Laura Welch. Laura, the schoolteacher, sat in her apartment, preferring good books to pool parties. George Bush and Laura Welch didn't meet. Strangely, Houston wasn't the first opportunity they had to meet, yet didn't. The same thing happened in Midland, Texas, where they grew up only a few blocks away from each other and even attended the same junior high school. They probably passed each other hundreds of times in both Midland and in Houston, but they never met.

In 1977 they sat in their respective apartments, both 31 and single, and all of their friends were married and most had families. Time was racing by, but neither had found that one special person. Mutual friends finally brought them together at a barbecue in Midland. Laura was then a librarian, and George was starting his first political campaign. Their friends thought that they might have been too different to be attractive to each other, but they needn't have worried. George made her laugh (not an easy trick with a librarian) and Laura made his eyes pop. George said that she was a great listener and since he was a great talker, it was a perfect fit. It must have been, because three weeks later they were engaged and in less than three months they were married.

Laura Bush, a former schoolteacher and librarian, has focused her effort on early childhood development, education reform and federal assistance to public libraries.

George and Laura Bush dancing at their Inaugural Ball.

Laura had a sheltered, loving childhood, and responded by being a loving, easy-going child. She grew up in the Methodist church, singing in the choir, and attending church with her family. Her mother taught Sunday school, and took her to swimming lessons and Girl Scouts. Laura loved reading and knew from grade school that she wanted to be a teacher or a librarian.

But the idyllic childhood and all the hopes and dreams of a young girl were soon shattered. Tragedy struck Laura and Midland shortly after her 17th birthday. She was driving with friends on a country road and accidentally ran a stop sign and broadsided another car. The driver in the other car died at the scene. He was a close friend of Laura's, and she collapsed. She was overcome with remorse and guilt. It took years before she would realize that she had no choice but to go on with life, but she still lives with that memory.

Just two weeks after the crash, Texas and the nation had its own tragedy: President Kennedy was assassinated in Dallas. Laura stumbled through her senior year, but a pensive, subdued, much older person had replaced the lively, smiling coed. Laura entered Southern Methodist University in 1964 and four years later graduated with a degree in education. She started teaching school in Dallas and then in Houston and Austin.

In 1994 George W. Bush was elected governor of Texas. As the first lady of Texas, Laura worked to enhance the reading skills of its citizens, particularly children. She instituted an initiative to help adults help pre-school children prepare for reading and learning when they entered school. She hosted fund-raisers for the public libraries. She promoted tourism, the arts, historic preservation, and volunteerism. She was vocal advocate for women's health and Alzheimer's disease.

George W. Bush won a hotly contested election and took office in 2001. The Bush's first years in the White House were not easy with the country devastated by the deadliest terrorist attack in our history and the decision to go to war in Iraq. The home front has been quieter, with Laura working to keep her daughters out of the media and get them both through college. Laura herself has concentrated on literacy and education, and is viewed as a wonderful helpmate and partner to her husband. She has been the faithful, calming influence, the "comforter in Chief" that the White House and the whole country has needed.

Lessons From Laura

Through the LORD's mercies we are not consumed, Because His compassions fail not. They are new every morning; Great is Your faithfulness. "The LORD is my portion," says my soul, "Therefore I hope in Him." (Lamentations 3:22).

Laura's lesson is that she is a more valuable helpmate for her husband because she activley joined his family and her famous in-laws. Her father-in-law has been president. Her mother-in-law has been First Lady. And her brother-in-law is the governor of Florida. She no doubt benefits from being in relationship with them. She learns much from their experience and counsel, so that she can support her husband more effectively.

One of the greatest lessons of Laura Bush is that tragedy doesn't define our lives. Our lives define how we handle tragedy. Few of us can imagine what it would feel like to accidentally take the life of a friend. Handling it must have been doubly hard for a teenaged girl. But somehow Laura rose above the guilt and pain. She speaks of it very little, so we can only guess that God's forgiveness and her consequent ability to forgive herself factored into her healing. It's a good guess. Instead of giving in to grief from which she could not rise, she honored her friend's life by making her own count. She honored God's plan for her by not quitting. She rose. She even found joy again. "It is never too late for a happy childhood."

Dear God, grant us wisdom and courage. Remind us, yet again, that all things are possible in You. You put people in our lives to lift and assist us. And when we come to You in prayer, there is always an answer. Amen

First Ladies National Historic Site in Canton, Ohio

When one thinks of the National Park Service and the U.S. Department of the Interior, one thinks of canyons and caves, forests and ferns, ravines and rivers. But within the National Park Service is a decidedly civilized attraction: a treasure trove of marble staircases, alabaster lights, feathered fans, beaded gloves and ball gowns, and oak shelves lined with books about amazing women— the First Ladies of the United States.

In Canton, Ohio, historians, a private non-profit partner, and park rangers have combined efforts and considerable resources to give a gift to the American public: the First Ladies National Historic Site. It features the meticulously restored former home of First Lady Ida Saxton McKinley and her husband, President William McKinley. In the next block is the National First Ladies' Library Education and Research Center, a library and archive devoted to the women who have served beside the presidents of the United States. Much of the research for this book was done there.

The McKinley's home, as charming as gingerbread and festooned with bunting, is called the "Saxton House." Costumed docents lead visitors from floor to floor, introducing them to Canton's famous First Family and pointing out architectural details that speak to a time gone by when craftsmanship was a labor of love. The net effect is one of time travel. It's almost possible to hear music from the small piano in the parlor and the ringing ping of fine china in the dining room as the McKinley family goes about their daily lives. The visitor is drawn into the triumph of winning a presidency and the tragedy of losing children to death. And more important, we are given an intimate glimpse into the private life of Ida, a First Lady who was altogether human. Today, in an age of public relations and polished media images, when it's easy to forget that celebrity does not render a person immune to trial and sorrow, there's something stunning about being introduced to Ida Saxton McKinley and all her imperfections. One wonders, then, about the other First Ladies. Did they ... does she ... struggle, too?

A quick walk answers the question ... and nearly any other pertaining to the First Ladies of the United States. The National First Ladies' Library Education and Research Center is a block away. Built in 1895, the seven-story, 20,000 square foot building was formerly the City National Bank, but now houses a research library, exhibits, a jewel box of a theater, an archive of First Ladies' belongings and clothing, and areas for meetings. Each of the floors is named for one of Ohio's seven First Ladies: lower level for Florence Harding, first floor for Helen Taft, second floor for Ida McKinley, third floor for Caroline Harrison, fourth floor for Lucretia Garfield, fifth floor for Lucy Hayes, and sixth floor for Anna Harrison.

The building itself is as spectacular as its contents. Dr. Sheila A. Fisher, Vice President of the National First Ladies' Library, designed the interiors of the building to honor the grace and style, character and strength of the ladies. Victorian opulence envelops 21st century visitors, and transforms the workaday world into an appointment with splendor. It's an incredible experience from the moment one ascends the front steps and opens the windowed doors. From the White Correra marble wainscot to the buttoned light switches, no detail has been overlooked. Everyone who enters stands a little straighter, softens the voice, and refines the manner. Clearly, the visitor is somewhere very special.

The building and its contents are almost eclipsed by the staff, people who are passionate about the First Ladies and their frequently unsung contributions to our nation's history. The staff is knowledgeable, gracious, generous, and hospitable. The formal surroundings are made friendly and the guests are made welcome by plainspoken, smiling people. Just like the White House.

Both the Saxton House and the First Ladies' Library are must-sees for visitors to Canton, Ohio ... or for anyone who wants to fully understand the vital and undeniable role women have played in the development of the United States of America.

The Ida Saxton McKinley House
331 Market Avenue South
Canton, Ohio
44702
Telephone 330-452-0876
Fax 330-456-3414

The First Ladies' Library Education and Research Center
205 Market Avenue South
Canton, Ohio
44702
Telephone 330-452-0876
Fax 330-445-2008

Selected Bibliography

Adler, Bill. *America's First Ladies*. New York: Taylor Trade Publishing. 2002.

Akers, Charles W. *Abigail Adams - An American Woman*. Boston: Little, Brown and Company. 1980.

Anderson, Christopher. *George and Laura - Portrait of an American Marriage*. New York: HarperCollins Publishers, Inc. 2002.

Anthony, Carl Sferrazza. *First Ladies - The Saga of the Presidents' Wives and Their Power 1789-1961*. New York: William Morrow and Company, Inc. 1990.

Anthony, Katharine. *Dolly Madison - Her Life and Times*. New York. Doubleday. 1949.

Baker, Jean H. *Mary Todd Lincoln - A Biography*. New York: W.W. Norton and Company. 1987.

Barbara Bush: *A Memoir*. New York, Charles Scribner's Sons, 1994.

Barzman, Sol. *The First Ladies*. New York: Cowles Book Company, Inc. 1970.

Boller, Paul F. Jr. *Presidential Wives*. New York: Oxford University Press. 1988.

Brandon, Dorothy, *Mamie Doud Eisenhower, A Portrait of a First Lady*. New York, Charles Scribner's Sons, 1954.

Bryan, Helen. *Martha Washington*. New York: John Wiley & Sons, Inc. 2002.

Caroli, Betty Boyd. *First Ladies*. New York: Oxford University Press. 1987.

David, Lester and Irene. *Ike and Mamie - The Story of the General and His Lady*. New York: G.P. Putnam's Sons. 1981.

Diller, Daniel C. and Stephen L. Robertson. *The Presidents, First Ladies, and Vice Presidents - White House Biographies 1789-1989*. Washington D.C.: Congressional Quarterly, Inc. 1989.

Eisenhower, Julie Nixon. *Special People*. New York, Simon and Schuster, 1977.

Felix, Antonia. *Laura America's First Lady, First Mother*. MA: Adams Media Corp. 2002.

Gelles, Edith B. *Abigail Adams A Writing Life*. New York: Routledge. 2002.

Gelles, Edith B. *Portia - The World of Abigail Adams*. Bloomington: Indiana University Press. 1992.

Gordon, Lydia. *From Lady Washington to Mrs. Cleveland*. Boston: Lee and Shepard Publishers. 1889.

Gould, Lewis. *American First Ladies - Their Lives and Their Legacy*. New York. Routledge. 2001.

Hay, Peter. *All the Presidents' Wives - Anecdotes of the Women Behind the Men in the White House*. New York: Viking Penguin Inc. 1988.

Heyman, C. David. *A Woman Named Jackie*. New York: Carol Communications. 1989.

Holloway, Laura C. *The Ladies of the White House; or In the Home of the Presidents*. Philadelphia: Bradley and Company. 1882.

Kilian, Pamela. *Barbara Bush - Matriarch of a Dynasty*. New York: St. Martin's Press. 2002.

King, Norman. *Hillary - Her True Story*. New York. Carol Publishing Group. 1993.

Maggio, Rosalie. *The New Beacon Book of Quotations by Women*. Boston. Beacon Press. 1996.

Means, Marianne. *The Woman in the White House - The Lives, Times and Influence of Twelve Notable First Ladies*. New York: Random House. 1963.

McConnell, Jane and Burt. *Our First Ladies*. New York: Thomas Crowell Co. 1961.

Osborne, Claire G., editor. *The Unique Voice of Hillary Clinton - A Portrait in Her Own Words*. New York: Avon Books. 1997.

Paletta, Lu Ann. *The World Almanac of First Ladies*. New York. Pharos Books. 1990.

Radcliffe, Donnie. *Hillary Rodman Clinton - A First Lady for Our Time*. New York: Warner Books. 1993.

Russell, Jan Jarboe. *Lady Bird - A Biography of Mrs. Johnson*. New York: Scribner. 1999.

Sadler, Christine. *America's First Ladies*. New York: Macfadden-Bartell. 1963.

Sferrazza, Anthony, editor. *This Elevated Position ... - A Catalogue And Guide To The National First Ladies' Library And The Importance Of First Lady History*. Canton, Ohio: National First Ladies' Library. 2003.

Thane, Elswyth. *Washington's Lady*. Mattituck, NY: Aeonian Press. 1977.

Truman, Margaret. *First Ladies*. New York: Random House. 1995.

West, J.B. *Upstairs at the White House - My Life With The First Ladies*. New York: Coward, McCann & Geoghegan, Inc. 1973.

Whitton, Mary Ormsbee. *First First Ladies 1789-1865*. New York: Hastings House. 1948.

Wikander, Lawrence E and Ferrell, Robert H. *Grace Coolidge - An Autobiography*. Wyoming. The Calvin Coolidge Memorial Foundation. 1992.